BINDWEED

WRITTEN BY
MARTHA LOADER

Bindweed was first performed at the Mercury Theatre, Colchester, on 13 June 2024 in a co-production between Mercury Theatre, HighTide and New Wolsey Theatre, in association with The Royal Exchange Theatre, Manchester.

The production subsequently ran at the New Wolsey Theatre, Ipswich, from 28 – 29 June and the Arcola Theatre, London, from 9 – 13 July.

The first draft of the play was presented as a Mercury Reads playreading event in 2022 and won the Judges' Award at the Bruntwood Prize for Playwriting 2022.

BINDWEED

WRITTEN BY
MARTHA LOADER

Nina, Siobhan, Belinda	Josie Brightwell
Mike, Ed	Simon Darwen
Peter, Charlie	Shailan Gohil
Jen	Laura Hanna
Brian, Alistair	Sean Kingsley
Frank	Moray Treadwell
Director	Jennifer Tang
Designer	Lulu Tam
Lighting Designer	Ric Mountjoy
Sound Designer / Composer	Jasmin Kent Rodgman
Dramaturg	Clare Slater
Movement Director	Jennifer Jackson
Fight Director	Ruth Cooper-Brown of Rc-Annie Ltd
Casting Support	Marc Frankum
	Hannah Miller
Assistant Director*	Chani Merrell
Production Mental Health Support	Applause for thought
Production Well-being Practitioner	Victoria Abbott

Production Team (for Mercury Theatre)

Senior Producer	Dilek Latif
Producer	Jenny Moore
Production Manager	Jeremy Naunton
Head of Construction	Philip Attwater
Deputy Workshop Manager	Harriet Bonner
Workshop Assistant	Jim Bonner
Freelance Carpenter	Rob van der Parker
Freelance Scenic Artist	David Thomas
Costume Supervisor	Chantelle Regan
Wardrobe Manager	Corinna Vincent
Company Stage Manager	Rebecca Samuels
Deputy Stage Manager	Lucy Quinton
Assistant Stage Manager	Gillian McGrath
Freelance Assistant Stage Manager	Marjanne van der Parker
Technical Manager	Luke McCann
Senior Technician	Roger Mills Lewis
Technical Team	Charlotte Beeby, Sam Copus, Hazuki Mogan, Alex Ray
Photography	Bea Maynard, Will Green
Marketing Lead	Nathan Garwood
Marketing Team	Rhianna Howard, Bea Maynard, Molly Richardson

* 6 month placement through the Birkbeck, University of London Director's Scheme

Cast

Josie Brightwell | Nina, Siobhan, Belinda

Josie trained at The Central School of Speech and Drama – BA (Hons) Acting.

Credits include: Judy Porter in BBC's **Call The Midwife**; Alison in **Mum's The Word: UK Tour**; Spa assistant in **Michael McIntyre's Big Show**; Factory Girl in **Les Misérables**; Eulampia Petrovna in **Black Snow** at the Moscow Art Theatre; **The Emperor of the Moon** workshop at NT Studio; **Made in Dagenham 10th Anniversary Concert** at The Palladium; Peggy in **The War of the Worlds**; Baba Yaga in **Hansel and Gretel** and Flora in Tennessee Williams' **27 Wagons Full of Cotton**.

Simon Darwen | Mike, Ed

Theatre credits include: **Of Mice and Men** (Birmingham Rep/Leeds Playhouse); **Beginning**, **The Invincibles** and **A Different Class** (Queens Theatre Hornchurch); **Sirens** (Mercury Theatre); **After Birth** (North Wall); **Missing People** (Leeds Playhouse/National Theatre Tokyo); **Skellig** (Nottingham Playhouse); **Much Ado About Nothing** (Jamie Hendry Productions/NESC/International Tour); **The Here and This and Now** (Plymouth Drum/Southwark Playhouse); **The Pitmen Painters** (New Vic); **Our Country's Good** (Out of Joint); **Lizzie Siddal** (Arcola); **The Armour/Hotel Plays** (Defibrilator); **Flare Path** (national tour); **Catch 22** (Northern Stage); **Virgin** (Watford Palace); **King Lear** (Theatre Royal Bath); **Mad About The Boy** (Young Vic/Bush Theatre); **SourLips** (Oval House); **The Fifth Column**, **The Taming of the Shrew** and **What the Women Did** (Southwark Playhouse); **Love Love Love** (Original Cast, Paines Plough); **Unrestless** (Old Vic Tunnels); **Accolade** (Original Revival Cast, Finborough Theatre); **Ramshackle Heart** (Public Theatre New York); **Arse** and **Shove** (Theatre503); **Mad Forest** and **The Wonder** (BAC); **The Merchant of Venice**, **The Tragedy of Thomas Hobbes**, **The Taming of the Shrew** and **A Midsummer Night's Dream** (RSC); **Fanny & Faggot** (Trafalgar Studios); **Nikolina** and **Bedtime for Bastards** (nabokov).

Television credits include: **Top Boy**; **Years and Years**; **Britannia**; **Call the Midwife**; **Silent Witness**; **The Bletchley Circle** and **The Bill**.

Film credit: **The Great Escaper** (released 2023).

Simon has also recorded numerous audiobooks and radio plays.

Shailan Gohil | Peter, Charlie

Shailan trainined at Bird College of Dance, Music & Theatre Performance.

Theatre includes: **Love's Labour's Lost** (RSC); **Mother Goose** (UK Tour); **Jack Absolute Flies Again** (Royal National Theatre); **Sunset Boulevard** (Royal Albert Hall); **South Pacific** (Chichester Festival Theatre); **Mamma Mia!** (West End, Novello Theatre) and **Dick Whittington** (Qdos Entertainment).

Laura Hanna | Jen

Training: The London Academy of Music & Dramatic Art (LAMDA)

Theatre credits include: **The Comedy of Errors** (Shakespeare's Globe Theatre); **Hakawatis: Women of the Arabian Nights** (Sam Wanamaker Theatre/Shakespeare's Globe); **Once Upon A Time in Nazi Occupied Tunisia** (Almeida); **Living Newspaper Edition 5** (Royal Court Theatre); **Signal Fires** (Fuel Theatre); **KaraOkay** (Bunker Theatre); **A History of Water in the Middle East** (Royal Court Theatre); **The Sweethearts** (The Finborough Theatre**)**; **A Bright Room Called Day** (Southwark Playhouse); **Lean** (Strip Theatre/Tristan Bates Theatre); **Beasts and Beauties** (Hampstead Theatre).

Television credits include: **Heartstopper** (Netflix) and **Casualty** (BBC).

Sean Kingsley | Brian, Alistair

West End: Aleksandr Voloshin in **Patriots** (Noel Coward Theatre); Ursus in **The Grinning Man** (Trafalgar Studios), Jean Valjean in **Les Misérables** (Queens/Palace Theatres); George in **The Drowsy Chaperone** (Novello); Braithwaite in **Billy Elliot** (Victoria Palace); Tom Jenkins in

Scrooge (Dominion), Admetus in **Cats** (New London) and **Me and My Girl** (Adelphi).

Other theatre includes: Aleksandr Voloshin in **Patriots** (Almeida); Kobus in **Mandela** (Young Vic); Mal in **The Addams Family** (UK tour/London Palladium); Billy in **Once** (New Wolsey); Ursus in **The Grinning Man** (Bristol Old Vic); **Oxy and the Morons** (New Wolsey); Annas in **Jesus Christ Superstar** (Regent's Park); Gyp Decarlo in **Jersey Boys** (UK tour); Max in **Jackie the Musical** (Dundee Gardyne); Khashoggi in **We Will Rock You** (tenth anniversary world tour); Judas in **Jesus Christ Superstar** (Minack); Eddie/Dr Scott in **The Rocky Horror Show** (European Tour); Frederick Trumper in **Chess, 20th Anniversary Concert** (Oslo); Bill Austin in **Mamma Mia!** (international tour); The Man in **Some Girls are Bigger than Others** (Lyric Hammersmith, national tour, Dublin); Mike in **Hot Pants** (Oldham Coliseum); Cyrano de Bergerac in **Cold Moon Rising**

(Jermyn Street); Tom Jenkins in **Scrooge** (national/european tours); Mike Costa in **A Chorus Line** (Derby Playhouse); Slap in **Hot Shoe Shuffle** (national tour); Gabey in **On the Town** (national tour); Joe in **Matchgirls** (Bromley); **A Month in the Country**, **The Rivals** and **Toad of Toad Hall** (Liverpool Playhouse) and **Fiddler on the Roof** (Liverpool Empire).

Notable workshops: **The Wall** (Roger Waters/Complicite) and **Martin Guerre** (Boublil and Schönberg/The Old Vic).

Actor/Musician: Merlin in **Sword in the Stone**; Sarah the Cook in **Dick Whittington**, Fleshcreep in **Jack & The Beanstalk** and King Camelot in **Sleeping Beauty** (Ipswich New Wolsey Rock Panto) and Orin in **Little Shop Of Horrors** (Birmingham Rep).

Film/TV: Tony in **Black Doves** (Netflix/Noisy Bear/Sister); Dave in **The Responder** (Dancing Ledge Productions); Alan in **London Road** (Cuba Pictures); PC Harrison in **Poirot** (LWT); Stuart Ambrose in **Wire in the Blood** (Coastal); Colin Piper in **Merseybeat** (BBC) and Gary Stephens in **The Bill** (Talkback).

Moray Treadwell | Frank

Theatre includes internationally: **The Beatles LOVE show** (Cirque Du Soleil/Apple, Las Vegas); **The Ruling Class** (English Theatre Frankfurt); **The Importance of Being Earnest** and **Corpse** (Vienna's English Theatre); **Rosencrantz and Guildenstern are Dead** (Moving Theatre/National Theatre of Macedonia) and **Waiting for Godot** (Italian tour, Il Palchetto/Good luck Prods).

In the UK: **The Railway Children** (Theatre Tracks, Kings Cross London/York Theatre Royal); **Macbeth** (Colchester Mercury); **Romeo and Juliet** (Theatre Royal, Bury St Edmunds); **Twelfth Night** (Contexture Theatre); **Wait Until Dark** and **The Little Foxes** (Perth Rep); **Amadeus**, **Cause Celebre**, **Absurd Person Singular**, **Charley's Aunt**, **Wuthering Heights** and **Man and Superman** (Pitlochry Festival Theatre); **The Caretaker** and **The Last Yellow** (Nuffield Theatre, Southampton). And national tours of: **Some Mother's Do 'Ave 'Em** (Limelight); **No Man's Land** and **Hysteria** (London Classic Theatre); **Arsenic and Old Lace** (Kenny Wax) and **Chitty Chitty Bang Bang** (Michael Rose).

Television includes: **The Witcher – Blood Origin** (Netflix); **EastEnders**, **Manchild**, **My Family**, **Murder Most Horrid** and **Beck** (BBC and associates); **Whose Baby?** (Channel 4); **Downton Abbey** (Carnival); **Planespotting** (Granada) and **Wuthering Heights** (LWT).

Film: **Don't Move** (Hammerstone, Capstone, Raimi Productions, Netflix); **Pirates of the Caribbean: Dead Man's Chest** (Bruckheimer/Disney); **Round Ireland with a Fridge** (Tony Hawks, Ed Bye) and **People We Hate at the Wedding** (Amazon).

Creatives

Martha Loader | Writer

Martha is a playwright, actor and producer from Ipswich. Previous work has been presented by HighTide, Mercury Theatre, Cambridge Junction, and INK. She is an associate artist of the New Wolsey Theatre, and is currently working on commissions from Menagerie Theatre Company, and the Almeida Theatre as part of the 'Genesis New Playwrights, Big Plays Programme'.

Bindweed was first written as part of the Mercury Playwrights scheme and won the Judges Award at the Bruntwood Prize for Playwriting 2022.

Jennifer Tang | Director

Jennifer is an award-winning theatremaker and stage director, specialising in making new work and fusing theatre with music. Jennifer trained at the University of East Anglia, the Young Vic and on the National Theatre Studio Director's course.

She was Genesis Fellow/Associate Director at The Young Vic Theatre 2020-22 and resident director for **Tina: The Tina Turner Musical** at the Aldwych Theatre.

Director selected work includes: **The Odyssey** (Unicorn Theatre); **The Tempest** (Regent's Park Open Air Theatre and Unicorn Theatre); **Further than the Furthest Thing**, **AI** and **The New Tomorrow** (Young Vic); **Gwei Mui/Ghost Girl** (Camdens People Theatre); **Mountains** (Royal Exchange and National Tour); **We Are You** (Young Vic, British Museum); **Clytemnestra** (The Gate); **Constellations** and **One Day When We Were Young** (Gest, Sweden).

Forthcoming/in Development: **Twine** (The Yard Theatre); **Fundamental** (NDT), and **Ghost Girl** for TV.

Lulu Tam | Designer

Lulu trained at the Royal Central of Speech and Drama, MA Scenography with distinction.

She is a teaching fellow at the University of Salford on TV, Film and Stage Design and a visiting lecturer at Royal Central of Speech and Drama.

Selected credits include: **Showdown** (Chamäleon Theater, Berlin); **I Really Do Think This Will Change Your Life** (Mercury Theatre); **Woodhill** (Edinburgh and UK tour); **The Killing of Sister George** (Told by An Idiot & New Vic Theatre); **Wáltsáil Abhaile** (An Taibhdhearc); **A Pretty Shitty Love** (Theatr Clwyd); **The Prince** (Southwark Playhouse); **This is Paradise** (Traverse Theatre); **Lit** (Nottingham Playhouse/High Tide Festival); **Seeds** (Pleasance Theatre); **Red/Chaos** (ArtsEd); **Invincible** (Stephen Joseph Theatre, UK Tour, Off-Broadway Tour) and **A Winter's Tale** (Les Kurbas Theatre, Ukraine).

Awards include: Linbury Prize (finalist); Taking the Stage, British Council (winner); World Stage Design 2017 and Naomi Wilkinson Award for Stage Design 2022 (winner).

Ric Mountjoy | Lighting Designer

Ric designs lighting for Theatre and Opera, and his work has been seen all over the world: at the Singapore International Arts Festival; in Seattle, Dubai, Doha and Dhaka; Hong Kong, Seoul, Guangzhou and Beijing, and most significantly in London and New York City.

Recent lighting designs include: **The Play that Goes Wrong** on Broadway (Lyceum Theatre), on a US National Tour, and in the West End (Duchess Theatre – Winner of the 2015 Olivier Award for Best New Comedy), also Australia & South Korea; **Lucrezia Borgia** and **Il Viaggio a Reims** (English Touring Opera); **Zog and the Flying Doctors** (Leeds Playhouse & National Tour); **The Government Inspector** (Marylebone Theatre); **Pinocchio** (Unicorn Theatre); **Father** by Akram Khan (Dhaka, Bangladesh); **God's Dice** by David Baddiel (Soho Theatre); **Uncle Vanya** (Theatr Clwyd & Sheffield Theatres); **Darbar Festival** (Akram Khan Company & Sadler's Wells Theatre); **Oi Frog + Friends** (West End); **Emancipation of Expressionism** (Boy Blue Entertainment, Barbican Theatre, & BBC TV); a site-specific **The Great Gatsby** (Theatr Clwyd); **Mr Popper's Penguins** (Seattle, Minneapolis, New York City & West End); the World Premiere of **Karagula** by Philip Ridley (site specific, Soho Theatre) and **What the Ladybird Heard** (West End & International Touring). For years he lit site-specific theatre for the company Slung Low, including **The White Whale** – an outdoor adaptation of Moby Dick (Leeds) and **Pandemic** (Singapore).

Ric worked for many years at English National Opera, and before that for Birmingham Royal Ballet.

ricmountjoy.com

Jasmin Kent Rodgman | Sound Designer/Composer

British-Malaysian Artist & Composer Jasmin brings together the contemporary classical, electronics and sound art worlds to create powerful soundscapes and musical identities. A collaborator across various art forms including dance, word, film and VR, her music often explores otherness, memory and plays with a sense of narrative.

Her music and live productions have been performed across the UK and internationally with partners such as Southbank Centre, London Fashion Week, World Music Festival Shanghai, Edinburgh International Festival, Wilderness Festival, the Roundhouse, Shoreditch Town Hall, Barbican, and the Royal Albert Hall. Her film scores have featured at festivals such as Sundance, SXSW, Toronto International Film Festival and the London Short Film Festival.

Previous theatre includes: **Julius Caesar** (Royal Shakespeare Company); **Titus Andronicus** (Shakespeare's Globe); **Paradise Now** (Bush Theatre); **Brown Girls Do It Too** (Soho Theatre); **Britannicus** (Lyric Hammersmith – Composer and Sound Designer); **Red Ellen** (Northern Stage – Composer & Sound Designer); **Prisoner C33** (BBC & Pioneer

Productions – Composer); **Dorian** (Reading Rep – Sound Designer); **Missing Julie** (Theatre Clywd – Composer and Sound Designer); **Nanjing** (Feature Film – Composer); **Harm** (BBC Film – Composer and Sound Designer, with a live production at Bush Theatre, London; **Somehow** (Music Theatre Wales); **Nineteen Ways of Looking** (Chinese Arts Now); **At Home with the World** (Bagri Foundation) and **The Spell & the Promise** (London Symphony Orchestra).

Clare Slater | Dramaturg

Clare is the Artistic Director and CEO of HighTide.

She was previously the Head of New Work at the Donmar Warehouse in London, where she worked on over thirty productions, including **The Trials** by Dawn King; **Love and Other Acts of Violence** by Cordelia Lynn; **Assembly** by Nina Segal; **Blindness** adapted by Simon Stephens; **[BLANK]** by Alice Birch; **Appropriate** by Branden Jacobs-Jenkins; **Berberian Sound Studio** adapted by Joel Horwood; **Sweat** by Lynn Nottage; **Silence** by Sonali Bhattacharyya, Gurpreet Kaur Bhatti, Ishy Din and Alexandra Wood; **Force Majeure** adapted by Tim Price; **The Resistible Rise of Arturo Ui** in a new version by Bruce Norris; **Limehouse** by Steve Waters; **The Lady from the Sea** in a new version by Elinor Cook; and **Becoming** by Michelle Terry and Rosalie Craig.

Other writing and dramaturg credits include: **Women in Power** dir. Blanche McIntyre (Nuffield, Southampton); **The Unknown Island** dir. Ellen McDougall, **Meet Your Neighbours** dir. Emily Lim, **Here's How It All Began** dir. Christopher Haydon, **Idomeneus** dir. Ellen McDougall (all for the Gate, Notting Hill); and **The Last Mermaid** dir. Bruce Guthrie with Charlotte Church (Wales Millennium Centre).

Clare previously worked as Executive Director of the Gate Theatre in Notting Hill and, prior to that, she was the Assistant Literary Manager at the National Theatre and worked in TV and film development with Rare Day. She also sits on the Creative Council of Shakespeare's Globe.

Jennifer Jackson | Movement Director

Jennifer is a Latinx British-Bolivian theatremaker, movement director and actor. Her acclaimed production, **Endurance**, premiered at HOME Manchester/ Battersea Arts Centre, and was shortlisted for the prestigious Stückemarkt at the Theatertreffen (Berliner Festspiele, 2022).

Theatre includes: **Work It Out** (HOME Manchester); **Cowbois** (Royal Shakespeare Company & Royal Court Theatre); **Julius Caesar** (Royal Shakespeare Company); **I, Joan**, **Macbeth** and **The Merchant of Venice** (Globe); **Britannicus** (Lyric Hammersmith); **The Breach** (Hampstead); **KES** (Bolton Octagon); **Five Children and It** (Theatre Royal Bath); **Endurance** (HOME Manchester/ Battersea Arts Centre); **The Mountaintop**, **Cuttin' it**, **Wuthering Heights**, **Death of a Salesman**, **Queens of the Coal Age** and **Our Town** (Royal Exchange Theatre); **Baby Reindeer** (Francesca Moody Productions/The Bush - Olivier

Award 2020); **Midnight Movie, Invisible Summer** and **Living Newspaper** (Royal Court); **Perspective** (New Views National Theatre); **Amsterdam** (ATC/Orange Tree/Theatre Royal Plymouth); **I Wanna Be Yours** (Paines Plough/The Bush); **Parliament Square** (Bush Theatre/Royal Exchange Theatre); **The Strange Undoing of Prudencia Hart** (New Vic Theatre); **Be My Baby** and **Around The World in 80 Days** (Leeds Playhouse); **Mountaintop** (UK Tour/Young Vic/ Desara Productions Ltd); **Mayfly** and **Out of Water** (Orange Tree).

Television and Film includes: **Hope – A film** (Clean Break); **Hold Hold Fire** (ICA, Olivia Plender) and **The Great** (Hulu).

Events include: **Coventry Moves**, Coventry City of Culture 2021.

Awards: She was a recipient of a Jerwood Live Work Award (2021) and was recently awarded the Jerwood New Work Fund (2023) for **WRESTLELADSWRESTLE**; Levehulme Arts Scholar 2019; MCGFutures Award; Oliver Award 2020 (**Baby Reindeer**).

Jennifer is the inaugural artist selected for The Artist Takeover (Factory International).

Ruth Cooper-Brown of Rc-Annie Ltd | Fight Director

Rc-Annie Ltd was established in 2005 by Ruth Cooper-Brown and Rachel Bown-Williams.

Theatre credits include: **Boys from the Black Stuff** (Liverpool Royal Court/National Theatre/West End); **Twelfth Night** (Regent's Park Theatre); **Minority Report** (NottinghamPlayhouse/Lyric Hammersmith); **Macbeth** (Donmar Warehouse & West End); **A Midsummer Nights Dream, Julius Caesar, The Empress, Richard III, Henry VI: Rebellion, Wars of the Roses, Henry VI Part 1** Open Rehearsal Project, **King John, Measure for Measure, As You Like It, The Taming of the Shrew, Tartuffe, The Duchess of Malfi, Salomé, Snow in Midsummer** (RSC); **Richard III, The Duchess of Malfi, A Midsummer Night's Dream, The Tempest, Hakawatis, Midsummer Mechanicals, I, Joan, Henry VIII, Julius Caesar, Romeo and Juliet, Playing Shakespeare with Deutsche Bank – Macbeth, Macbeth, Emilia, Othello, The Secret Theatre, Boudica, Lions and Tigers, Much Ado About Nothing, Twelfth Night, Comus and Imogen** (Shakespeare's Globe); **Lucia di Lammermoor** (Royal Opera House); **2:22 A Ghost Story** (West End and Tour); **Bronco Billy** (Charing Cross Theatre); **Great Expectations** (Royal Exchange); **The Pillowman** (Duke of York); **Crazy for You** (West End); **Linck & Mülhahn**, **'Night, Mother** (Hampstead); **Noises Off!** (Theatre Royal Bath/West End); **Oklahoma** (Young Vic/West End); **Newsies** (Wesley Troubadour) and **Baghdaddy** (Royal Court).

Marc Frankum | Casting Support

Marc originally trained as an actor at Drama Centre London before moving into casting.

Marc has cast **The Importance of Being Earnest, The Comedy of Errors, Baskerville, Aladdin, Moll Flanders, Pieces of String, Much Ado About Nothing, Clybourne Park, Noises Off** and **Macbeth** (Mercury Theatre, Colchester); **The Full Monty** (2023 UK Tour); **Sky Comedy Rep** (Birmingham Rep); **The Children** (Theatre Royal Bury St Edmunds); **The Walworth Farce** (Southwark Playhouse Elephant); **The Way Old Friends Do** (Birmingham Rep/UK Tour/West End); **Mother Goose** (Cambridge Arts Theatre); **The Play what I Wrote** (Birmingham Rep/UK Tour); **Now Is Good** (Storyhouse, Chester); **Bang Bang** (Northcott Theatre/UK Tour); **The History Boys** (Grand Theatre Wolverhampton); **Owners**, **Tonight at 8.30** and **Mother Adam** (Jermyn Street Theatre); **The Full Monty** (UK Tours); **The Band** (West End/UK Tour); **Calendar Girls** (UK Tour); **God of Chaos** and **The Kneebone Cadillac** (Theatre Royal Plymouth); **Dracula** (Touring Consortium Theatre Company); **Out of Order** (UK Tour); **Hand to God** (West End); **Dial M for Murder** (UK Tour); **The Duck House** (West End); **Goodnight Mister Tom** (West End/Chichester Festival Theatre/The Childrens Touring Partnership); **The Mousetrap** (60th Anniversary Tour); **The Woman in Black** (West End); **An Inspector Calls** (UK Tour) and many more.

Marc is also the in-house casting director for the English Theatre Frankfurt where he has cast **The Two Popes, Sylvia, Something Rotten, Now & Then, Suddenly Last Summer, Sister Act, Secret Life of Humans 2022, The Totalitarians, Young Frankenstein, The Girl on the Train, Switzerland, Secret Life of Humans, The Effect, Sweeney Todd, One Flew Over the Cuckoo's Nest, The Children, Apologia, Cabaret, The Lion in Winter, Jekyll & Hyde the Musical, Hand to God, Pygmalion, The Hound of the Baskervilles, Handbagged, Spamalot, The Picture of Dorian Gray, The Glass Menagerie, Disgraced, Death and the Maiden, Other Desert Cities, Ghost The Musical** and **Strangers on a Train**.

Hannah Miller CDG | Casting Support

Hannah was the RSC's Head of Casting from 2008-2022. Previously she worked as the Casting Assistant at the National Theatre, Deputy Head of Casting at the RSC and Casting Director for Birmingham Rep. She now works as a freelance Casting Director most recently working for the Royal Exchange theatre on productions of **Great Expectations** and **Brief Encounter,** and **My Neighbour Totoro** for the RSC. She is currently working with Wales Millenium Centre on a stage adaptation of **Pontypool** and Queen's Theatre, Hornchurch on **Bedroom Farce**. Hannah works with drama schools and industry organisations, advising actors on professional development and demystifying casting and directed the ArtsEd Actors final year showcase in both 2023 and 2024. She continues to work with the RSC's Creative Learning and Engagement team as an Associate Learning Practitioner and is an RSC Associate Artist.

Chani Merrell | Assistant Director

Chani is currently undertaking a master's degree in theatre

directing at Birkbeck College London and is the Resident Assistant Director at the Mercury. Theatre credits at the Mercury include **Sleeping Beauty**, **The Importance of Being Earnest** and **Midsummer**.

Other directing/performing credits include: **That Face** (Orange Tree Theatre); **The Resistible Rise of Arturo Ui** (Rose Bruford College); **How to Date a Feminist** (Corpus Playroom); **Cambridge Footlights Pantomime: Rapunzel** (ADC Theatre); **Little Shop of Horrors** (ADC Theatre); and **Ordinary Days** (ADC Theatre).

Applause for thought | Production Mental Health Support

Applause for thought is a multi-award winning community interest company that facilitates mental health support, talks and workshops, accredited training and bespoke consultancy and aims to create safe, empowering and empathetic spaces for all within the arts. Their mantra is 'Education Equals Prevention' as they believe that if they can empower individuals and organisations with the awareness, knowledge and tools surrounding mental health and make this information and support more accessible and affordable, they can not only help break the stigma around mental health, but they can also help prevent more serious mental health concerns from developing and contribute to cultural change that will make the arts a healthier and more inclusive industry to be a part of.

applauseforthought.co.uk

Victoria Abbott | Production Well-being Practitioner

Victoria is a Psychotherapist and Support Lead at Applause for thought. She has been working on BINDWEED as the Production Wellbeing Practitioner where she develops helpful resources for the company as well as actively supports all teams with their own mental health, resilience, and wellbeing as they work within the themes and content of the show.

MERCURY

MERCURY THEATRE

Mercury Theatre is the artistic powerhouse in the East – a vital, vibrant, welcoming centre of culture for the people of Colchester, Essex and beyond. The award-winning theatre presented in our auditorium and in our studio transforms and enriches the lives of our community. Through our Mercury Productions and Mercury Originals we produce world-class theatre, reinventing familiar stories and conjuring up bold, new ones. Our talent development programme seeks out fresh voices and stories that encourage people to see through the eyes of others. The Mercury's participation programmes connect communities and celebrate creative potential by providing people with everyday opportunities to be artistic and innovative.

A producing and receiving house with 530 seats in the theatre and a capacity of 96 in the studio, the newly (2021) refurbished Mercury is accessible throughout and boasts a thriving café-bar, dance studio, rehearsal space, participation space and impressive backstage workshop.

Following the major renovation in 2021, Mercury was awarded a BREEAM Very Good certificate, placing it in the top 25% of public buildings in the UK for environmental standards. In 2021 the Mercury was profiled by Theatre Trust as a model of good practice in the UK.

The Mercury was established in 1937, is registered Charity Number 232387 and receives regular investment from:

Premier Partners

mercurytheatre.co.uk
@MercuryTheatre

#MercuryForAll

HIGHTIDE

HighTide is a writer-centred theatre company, based in the East of England. We produce new plays by playwrights from our region, touring across the East and beyond. We run a year-round writer development programme that creates space for East of England playwrights to thrive. We offer creative writing programmes in schools and community groups to build confidence, wellbeing and employability. We are committed to ensuring everyone, from all backgrounds, can participate in the joy and power of theatre. We believe that partnership and collaboration makes better theatre, as well as more lasting, positive social change. HighTide holds the climate crisis in its name; a daily reminder of our responsibility to act now – with imagination and creativity. We see climate and social justice as inextricably linked and believe that theatre can help rehearse a better future for us all.

HighTides work is made possible by public investment in the arts from Arts Council England.

Principal Partner: Lansons | Team Farner

HighTide: 01473 459200 / hello@hightide.org.uk
Website | hightide.org.uk
Facebook | HighTideTheatre
Twitter | @_HighTide_
Instagram | @_hightideheatre_

THE NEW WOLSEY THEATRE

The New Wolsey Theatre is an award-winning theatre that enriches the lives of people living in Suffolk. We're a vibrant cultural hub offering a diverse range of performances, community engagement and artist development. We have a national reputation for excellence, diversity, and accessibility and are dedicated to delivering this essential work.

We make our own productions as well as co-produce with UK and international theatres and companies, and are renowned for staging world premieres and landmark revivals of musicals and plays which recently includes *Little Shop of Horrors*, *Brief Encounter*, *Kinky Boots*, *The Season* (recently transferring to the West End under the new title *Two Strangers (Carry a Cake Across New York)*), *The Time Machine* (recently nominated for an Olivier Award), *Feel Me, Boy On The Roof, The Red Lion,* and our iconic and award-winning Rock 'n' Roll pantomime. We also present productions by acclaimed national touring companies and we support the work of emerging theatre companies and independent artists.

The New Wolsey Theatre is partially funded by Arts Council England, Suffolk County Council, and Ipswich Borough Council and is supported by local business sponsors as well as corporate and private members. As a not-for-profit charity, we rely on their investment, and we are very grateful for their unwavering support that allows us to fulfil our mission.

Instagram, Twitter and Facebook: @NewWolsey
wolseytheatre.co.uk

ROYAL EXCHANGE THEATRE

The Royal Exchange Theatre transforms the way people see theatre, each other and the world around them. Our historic building was taken over by artists in 1976 and today it is an award-winning cultural charity that produces new theatre in-the-round, in communities, on the road and online.

Exchange remains at the heart of everything we make and do. Our currency is brand new drama and reinvigorated classics, the boldest artists and a company of highly skilled makers - all brought together in a shared imaginative endeavour to trade ideas and experiences with the people of Greater Manchester (and beyond).

The Exchange's unique auditorium is powerfully democratic, a space where audiences and performers meet as equals, entering and exiting through the same doors. It is the inspiration for all we do; inviting everyone to understand the past, engage in today's big questions, collectively.

@rxtheatre
royalexchange.co.uk

bruntwood

BRUNTWOOD PRIZE FOR PLAYWRITING

The Bruntwood Prize for Playwriting nurtures the voices of world-class writers. Born from a Manchester-based partnership between the Royal Exchange Theatre and property company Bruntwood, it is now the biggest playwriting prize in Europe.

At the core of the Prize is a genuine endeavour to discover new stories that change the way we think about the world around us. We want to empower anyone and everyone to enter. Our year-round programme of events, masterclasses and workshops are committed to helping playwrights develop their craft.

The Bruntwood Prize is now recognised as a launch-pad for some of the country's most respected and produced playwrights and screenwriters. In 2025, the Prize will be celebrating its 20th anniversary of searching for great new plays by the writers of tomorrow.

@bruntwoodprize
writeaplay.co.uk

Initial Run

Premiered at Mercury Theatre, Colchester
Thu 13 – Sat 22 Jun 2024

New Wolsey Theatre, Ipswich
Fri 28 – Sat 29 Jun 2024

Arcola Theatre, London
Tue 9 – Sat 13 Jul 2024

BINDWEED

Martha Loader

you fit into me
like a hook into an eye

a fish hook
an open eye

Margaret Atwood

Characters

JEN, *female, thirties*

BRIAN, *male, fifties*
MIKE, *male, forties*
FRANK, *male, seventies*
CHARLIE, *male, nineteen*
NINA, *female, thirties*

Members of the cast (except Jen) double for the following parts:
PETER, *male, thirties*
ALISTAIR, *male, sixties*
ED, *male, forties*
BELINDA, *female, seventies*
SIOBHAN, *female, forties*

Notes

A comma (,) indicates a pause when alone in a line.
A forward slash (/) indicates overlapping speech.
An elipsis (…) or no final punctuation, indicates a trailing-off.

This text went to press before the end of rehearsals and so may differ slightly from the play as performed.

PART ONE

Scene One

SIOBHAN *stands centre stage.*

BRIAN *enters and stands on one side of the stage.*

SIOBHAN *exits.*

BRIAN. Um, yup. I'm um, Brian. Davies. Brian Davies. Bri if you

Cough.

I

Where did you want me to start?

Oh. Yea.

Okay well we met, I guess, yea I guess we met pretty late on. For me. She'd been married, was married before. Had a kid. Kid before that too from another

Yea.

So two, two kids. Only small.

But I

Never really

You know.

Busy with work I guess and

My dad was ill for a while.

Didn't really think I'd meet anyone. Thought, you know, thought it would probably just be me. Which was fine. Like my own company, you know. Don't massively. Not massively er, sociable. Yea.

I work in printing. In an office. Pretty big office. The others are alright. Get on my nerves a bit, you know. Colleagues are... yea.

And she, well she was new then. Got a job in

Well it's confusing, cos it's not just our company in the office, there's other

Yea, so.

She worked in recruitment. And they, they, their company set up in our office. So printing and recruitment.

She, we met, there was a coffee machine in the shared kitchen. We shared a kitchen. All of us. And the coffee machine was one of those, just impossible to use, you know? So none of us did. Just this fancy-arse coffee machine that no one knew how to work. And I went into the kitchen one day and there she was using the coffee machine and I said, well I said, 'How'd you do that?', and she said, 'What?' and I said, 'How'd you get it to work?', and she said, 'I put a coffee pod in.' Like I knew what a coffee pod was. And well, turns out, we'd been trying to put loose coffee in when we were meant to... We'd been opening the pods and pouring the coffee into the

So it didn't work.

But her sister had the exact same at home, she said.

She laughed then. Not cruel. She wasn't, not like that. I thought maybe it was at me, but it wasn't. She's got this laugh, see, she does it when she's nervous. Laughs and laughs. Then stops suddenly and gets all embarrassed.

So then, well yea I think, I think I kept following her into the kitchen each... not in a stalker way, just

Yea.

And she'd say – 'Ey up, it's two sugars again' each time I came in. Cos I have two

And then one day a few people were going to the pub, so we.

We went to the pub too and haven't spent a day apart from each other since.

Pause.

And then, little while back, it was our anniversary. Four years. And she said she was leaving. Taking the kids. Did that little, that little laugh thing. That laugh that I'd always loved so much. That laugh she does when she's nervous. But this time it felt like that laugh was a knife to the heart. And yea, so yea, I grabbed the back of her head and smashed it into the top of the kitchen island. Just to stop her laughing you know.

Pause.

And leaving too I guess.

Scene Two

A bar.

JEN *and* PETER *sit on velvet-covered stools.*

A couple of drinks between them.

JEN*'s is nearly gone.*

PETER. Concrete.

JEN. Sorry?

PETER. For the kitchen island? I went for polished concrete? I was going to go for marble but I thought, so early 2000s, you know?

JEN. Oh?

PETER. Yea. Looks really sleek actually. What's yours, not marble is it? Always putting my foot in it.

JEN. My

PETER. Island. Your counters.

JEN. I don't have a kitchen island.

Barely have a kitchen, to be honest.

PETER. Well, you know, just a thought. If you wanted to upgrade. Most of the properties I work on, they just stick some cheap laminate counter on. But I guess they know everyone who buys these places is just going to rip out the kitchen and put a new one in.

JEN. Oh, yea, right.

PETER. Should sell them without kitchens really. Kitchens and bathrooms. People are only going to want to put in their own. But, you know, that would be mad.

Do you own your own place?

JEN. No. I rent.

PETER. Expensive I bet. I've heard Colchester's on the up.

JEN. Is it?

PETER. Sure. Best to get on the property ladder as soon as you can. They're all piling out of London. This place will be full of banker wankers before you know it.

JEN. I'll bear that in mind.

JEN drains her glass.

Slight pause.

PETER. Lived here long?

JEN. Moved back recently. I was living in London for a while but

I

,

My parents are near the Suffolk border, so it was here or Ipswich really. And, well…

PETER. This whole area seems, yea, seems all right actually. My family's in the arse end of Norfolk but I wanted to be closer to London. More jobs, more nightlife, more… well people really.

JEN. Sure.

PETER. Dating in Norfolk's like, *um are you my sister*?

Silence.

JEN. I might get another one. Do you – ?

PETER. Oh. Sure yea. I'll get these though, can't have you paying for everything.

JEN. It's fine.

PETER. No, no. Guys should pay.

JEN. Well not / really

PETER. / I'm old fashioned like that. Bit of a gent.

JEN. Uh huh.

Well I'll just

She stands.

get the ball rolling.

PETER. I think it's table service.

JEN. I'll just go to the bar. It's quicker.

PETER. I do think it's table service.

Pause.

JEN *sits.*

Pause.

So uh, yea. So what do you do?

JEN. Just started a new job actually.

PETER. Wow, oh right. How's that going?

JEN. Good, yea. Kind of the same thing I've been doing for a while now

PETER. Oh cool, right.

JEN. but hopefully with less of the bureaucracy. The bullshit. I've just finished the training, but the practical side will

PETER. Nice.

JEN. I'll start that soon.

PETER. Uh huh.

JEN. I mean, I reckon it'll be quite intense.

PETER. God yea, aren't new jobs always? Don't want to make a tit of yourself early on cos that's what people will remember you for forever.

JEN. Right, yea. I kind of meant more what I'll actually be doing / will be

PETER. / Yea, right, yea. There was this lad at my place, tripped over the front doorstep on his first day. Really nasty fall. Smashed his face into the carpet. Lost both his front teeth. Really nasty. Got called *Stu* from then on. You know, like the guy in *The Hangover* who loses his

JEN *shrugs*.

Think his name is actually like Kevin or something. Can't remember.

JEN. You don't know his name?

PETER. We've all got nicknames at work. It's like a right of passage.

JEN. Mm.

PETER. Like there's 'Ted' cos he's hairy as a bear. And Stevo's 'Stevo' because he looks like Steve Buscemi. He's got this condition which makes his eyes look really, you know

JEN. Jesus.

PETER. Right? And Franko

JEN. Is a fascist?

PETER. What? Oh, ha, no. He got so pissed one night he started walking like Frankenstein.

JEN. The scientist?

PETER. What?

PART ONE, SCENE TWO   11

JEN. The scientist was Frankenstein. The monster is

PETER. Yea sure right.

JEN. So what's yours?

PETER. My

JEN. Nickname.

PETER. Oh it's

   I can't remember.

JEN. Yes you can.

PETER. It's silly really.

JEN. Well now you have to tell me.

PETER. No it's just it's because

JEN. Come onnn.

PETER. No it's just

JEN. Peter.

PETER. It's Paedo.

   Silence.

JEN. Oh.

PETER. Not for any

JEN. Sure.

PETER. It's because of my name. Peter, *Paedo*. They called me Pedro for a while, but Paedo stuck I guess.

JEN. People at your actual place of work call you that?

PETER. Not in front of clients.

JEN. ,

   Well that sounds fun.

   Silence.

   Where is this waiter? I'm going to the bar.

PETER. No rush, is there?

JEN *doesn't reply.*

Go on then. I'll guess.

JEN. Guess?

PETER. What you do. I'll guess.

JEN. I think it was on my / profile

PETER. / School. You work in a school. Sixth form?

JEN. No.

PETER. Something like that though, no?

JEN. No.

PETER. Computer-based then. I'm right, aren't I?

JEN. Isn't everyone computer-based in some way?

PETER. Truckies. Landscape gardeners. Postmen.

JEN. Fine. Carry on then.

PETER. Give me a clue.

JEN. I did give you a clue. It says on my profile.

PETER. Ah yea, but just like your job title or something. That could mean anything. Everyone's so vague on there.

JEN. Not men. Men aren't vague.

PETER. No, right.

JEN. Give you their full work address sometimes. Picture of them outside their front door if you're lucky.

PETER. Ha, right.

JEN. Unless they have kids. Then they're vague.

You'll know if they *don't* have kids.

Then it's a picture of them holding a kid with a statement underneath saying 'not my kid'.

PETER. Ha, yea I guess it's

JEN. And dogs, and children in Africa, and grannies – 'Not my granny'. But if they do have kids, you'll find that out on the second date. Third maybe. They can do that, I suppose, more easily. Hide their kids.

PETER. Girls also

JEN. But where they work. God, yea. I could turn up at any number of workplaces just based on profile alone. Don't even need to have spoken to them.

Doubt women do that.

PETER. Well no exactly, that's what I'm saying. Bit weird, isn't it? Could just say where you work.

JEN. Ha yea, well I guess it's just a

Like a safety thing, right?

PETER. What?

JEN. Doesn't matter.

Silence.

PETER. Doesn't look like the waiter's coming back. Wanna finish these and go back to mine?

JEN. No, thank you.

PETER. I've got this really nice red on the go

JEN. No thank you.

PETER. An Argentinian Malbec

JEN. You're okay.

PETER. My dad swears by the Argenitian reds.

JEN. I think I might just go actually

PETER. Oh.

JEN. I've got an early

PETER. Right yea, god, me too.

JEN. It was nice to

PETER. Yea, yea and you. We should definitely

JEN. Mm.

PETER. Maybe next week. I could take you bowling. Or like, crazy golf or something.

JEN. Mm.

PETER. An activity date.

JEN. Yea. Yea, maybe.

PETER. Cool. Shall we look at diaries now or

JEN. I'll have to text you.

PETER. Oh yea, okay great. Mine's all digital now, got everything on my G-Cal, wouldn't know where I was without it.

JEN. It was nice to meet you, Peter.

PETER. Oh yea, and you, yea.

I'll just, I'll just stay and finish this quickly.

Scene Three

Community centre room.

PETER *becomes* CHARLIE.

The other men enter, bringing plastic chairs in with them.

They sit in a circle.

JEN *sits in the circle too.*

It is a democratic circle.

JEN *sits upright. In charge. In control.*

She smiles encouragingly at the group.

They don't smile back.

JEN. Well. It's great to have you all in one place. To start this part of the journey together as one cohort. To support and nurture each other as you move into the next stage of your journey. I'm Jen, I'll be your course facilitator for this part of the programme. I warn you now, it will be a difficult and, I'm sure, at times, frustrating and emotionally-taxing process. But ultimately this will be an extremely rewarding and, hopefully, life-changing

MIKE *raises his hand.*

JEN *notices but doesn't immediately respond.*

Life-changing experience.

MIKE. Question.

JEN. One moment please, Mike.

As much as this is about you as individuals – *learning, changing, doing the work* – this group is an equally integral part of the process. An opportunity to work together and support each other as peers as you advance in this

MIKE. Journey?

JEN. Yes, thanks Mike.

Advance in this journey.

MIKE. Question.

JEN. ,

Yes Mike.

MIKE. I was just wondering if you're planning on finishing on time tonight?

JEN. Well yes, that was the plan.

Can we

MIKE. Sure. It's just sometimes these things run over and I'm getting a lift.

JEN. Yes. I'm planning to finish on time.

MIKE. Great okay. Thanks.

JEN. Okay?

As I was saying

MIKE. Do you know the postcode?

JEN. You really needed to sort this before.

MIKE. That's okay, I'll look it up.

MIKE takes out his phone and starts texting.

JEN. Mike.

MIKE. Just a second.

JEN. Mike. We do ask that you don't

MIKE. Just a second. I'm just letting my lift know.

JEN. Okay, but it's actually really important

BRIAN. Do you think we'll finish on time every week? I also have a lift.

JEN. Yes. Okay? I will do my best to finish on time every week. But that will be up to you as well. How receptive you are to the work we're doing. As I was saying, this part of the programme is a really important part of your

MIKE clicks his phone off.

MIKE. Journey.

He puts it back in his pocket.

JEN. Yes. And in order to complete your

MIKE. Journey.

JEN. Mike.

FRANK. Yes, please stop interrupting, Michael.

MIKE. Mike.

FRANK. Mike. Apologies. But some of us are trying to listen.

PART ONE, SCENE THREE   17

MIKE. My *apologies*.

JEN. Thank you. Yes. This is a crucial part of the programme, to get you to really dig down into your past and find ways to change your behaviour going forwards.

You will need to work as a team, but the most crucial part is your own personal jour –

Process.

Okay?

Silence.

JEN *looks around at the group.*

They look back at her.

She breathes in. Then out.

Back in control.

Just to remind you all that this is a safe space. A place where a lot of very sensitive and private information will be disclosed by each of you each session, so we ask you to sign up to our confidentiality agreement which I'll just

JEN *pulls a stack of paper from beneath her seat.*

Gives it to FRANK *beside her to take and pass along.*

This is a sort of pledge to be honest and open in your own story, and generous and receptive to others with theirs. Nothing leaves the group, although if I have a concern that you are a danger either to yourself or others this may be escalated. There's a box to tick just at the bottom there to say you understand and agree to this.

MIKE. And what if we don't?

JEN. You have to as part of the requirements of the programme.

MIKE. Then why make us tick it if we don't have a choice?

JEN. Because, I suppose, well really you do have a choice. You always have a choice

CHARLIE. Prison.

JEN. Well not, not necessarily but yes, I suppose, for some of you, for some people not completing this course may result in you

So we just ask that you tick it.

FRANK. Are you new?

JEN. Well not, not

FRANK. It doesn't matter. I just wondered. We all start somewhere.

JEN. This is my first group here, but I've

FRANK. That's nice. Isn't that nice?

MIKE *snorts*.

BRIAN. Seems a bit risky. This is, there's a lot riding on this for me.

JEN. I've worked in lots of equivalent settings.

MIKE. What are *equivalent settings*?

JEN. Look, my CV is not what's / important.

BRIAN. / With all due respect Jen, your CV actually is quite important. We've all got a lot riding on this.

MIKE. Yea, rather not be one of your guinea pigs, thanks.

JEN. That's not

MIKE (*to* BRIAN). Might as well have 'L' plates dangling from her

JEN. Can we just get back to where / we

CHARLIE. / My mum was a nurse.

JEN. Oh.

Okay, well that's

CHARLIE. I just, I know about confidentiality from her. Everyone does it now.

JEN. Right. Exactly.

PART ONE, SCENE THREE   19

CHARLIE. Have to tick boxes like this all the time.

JEN. Right.

CHARLIE. Doesn't really mean anything.

JEN. Right. Well no. I mean, it does actually mean quite a lot. It's very import –

CHARLIE. Make you sign stuff like this at the gym and like, if you buy a car.

FRANK (*sincere*). Do they?

MIKE (*incredulous*). *Do* they?

CHARLIE. Think so. Dunno. Maybe that's

Doesn't matter.

JEN. No but, that's right Charlie. Lots of people do ask that you maintain confidentiality in

BRIAN. Where we have to put our address...?

JEN. Yes.

BRIAN. Do we put current address or our, y'know, main address?

JEN. Well just where you're living now.

BRIAN. Okay, it's just I'm not sure how long I'll be where I am now because I won't be able to afford it much longer what with the

And my friend said they could probably put me up if it came to it so...

JEN. Just where you are now.

MIKE. It says 'current address' mate.

BRIAN. Right, yea, I get that. I'm just saying I don't know how long my current address will be *current*, cos I'm having to think about maybe moving soon.

JEN. Well you will need to update us if you do end up moving because our records need to be up to date.

BRIAN. Yea, I *get* that, which is why I'm saying that my current address might not *be* my current address for much longer.

MIKE. All right mate, calm down. Just a simple question.

BRIAN. Well it's not a simple question for me, is it? Because of what I'm just explaining.

MIKE. Sounds pretty / simple to me.

JEN. / Okay. Thank you both. Brian, just put down where you are tonight and underneath you can put your friend's address just in case.

BRIAN. I don't know my friend's address. That's the problem.

JEN. Okay, well if you

BRIAN. I know his street name. I could maybe find his house on Google Street View.

JEN. That's not necessary.

BRIAN. It would just take a minute. My friend Kev showed me how to do it.

JEN. You can do it at the end of the session. Right now

BRIAN. But I'm getting a lift so

JEN. Brian. Just not now, okay?

CHARLIE. Street View is actually pretty handy. Can't remember an exact address, but know what the front door looks like or like vaguely where it is on the road, you can usually work it out.

MIKE. Cos that doesn't make you sound like a fucking stalker, mate.

CHARLIE. I'm not a fucking

I was just saying.

JEN. Yes, okay, let's just

Let's move on, shall we?

CHARLIE. No, cos he's calling me a fucking stalker.

MIKE. Said you sounded like one mate, not that / you are one.

CHARLIE. / I'm not your mate, *mate*.

JEN. Okay.

MIKE. Fine by me, *mate*.

FRANK. Oh this is ridiculous.

MIKE. All right Father Fuck, butt out would you?

FRANK. I'd prefer it if you made an effort to control your language.

JEN. / Yes, can we all just

MIKE. / Control my language? Oh I'm sorry, is God offended by my blasphemy?

FRANK. No, I am.

MIKE. Cock shit arse cunt.

JEN. Mike.

MIKE. Twat dick fuck cumhole.

FRANK. Better?

MIKE. Yea, actually.

JEN. Okay.

MIKE. Tit.

JEN *stands*.

JEN. Okay.

Let's just get something clear shall we? While you are here, you play by my rules. The rules of this programme. And that means no incendiary language. No fighting. No... *twatting about*. Okay?

That goes for all of you.

Otherwise I will fail you all and believe me that will look extremely bad in a court of law.

Clear?

BRIAN, CHARLIE *and* FRANK *nod*.

MIKE *is silent*.

Mike?

Clear?

MIKE. Crystal.

CHARLIE *smacks* MIKE *in the mouth*.

The room is shocked.

CHARLIE. Sorry.

Thought he swore again.

Scene Four

BRIAN *becomes* ALISTAIR.

The other men exit.

ALISTAIR. Well it sounds like you had a lively session.

JEN. Oh god Alistair, I did, I had it under control, they just

ALISTAIR. Mm yes.

JEN. I mean, I imagine group dynamics are always

ALISTAIR. Yes.

JEN. difficult to get the balance right at first but

ALISTAIR. Look, Jen. It's fine. We've all had similar experiences.

JEN. Have you?

ALISTAIR. Well no, this is most probably because you're a woman. And they don't respect women.

JEN. Right.

ALISTAIR. But it wasn't a very successful job callout so

JEN. Oh.

ALISTAIR. You were by far the best candidate for the role, Jen, don't get me wrong. But some hulking great guy would gain their respect from the off. You're just going to have to work a lot harder and there's no getting around it.

JEN. Of course. Yea. I'm used to men being

I mean I used to have handcuffs and a taser but

ALISTAIR. Ha! Right.

JEN. But no, I've got this.

ALISTAIR. I'm sure.

Now. We've got a huge waiting list for this programme, so do you want to throw any of the men off the group after what happened or are you happy to continue with them?

The thing I will say is that obviously there's a reason they're all here in the first place and quite possibly you wouldn't find anyone less *unruly* to replace them with.

JEN. Yea that's

ALISTAIR. It's also a fuckload of paperwork.

JEN. Oh. Sure.

ALISTAIR. So, up to you. But my advice would be to stick with what you've got for now.

JEN. Absolutely. I can handle them.

ALISTAIR. I have no doubt.

Now, obviously these last few months of the programme trial are fully funded, but our other funding continues to be slashed to buggery. Who knows. They might decide it's all worthwhile and fund another year or two.

JEN. Hopefully.

ALISTAIR. We like to live life on the edge in this industry, Jen. Job security and programme sustainability are for suckers.

JEN. Ha. Right. Yea.

ALISTAIR. Great. Good job, Jen. You're going to be terrific, I know it.

JEN. Thank you.

ALISTAIR. I'll just need you to write a quick incident report before you go. You've been shown how to lock up, haven't you?

JEN. Um yes I think, on my first day they

ALISTAIR. Wonderful. Do join us at the pub quiz tonight if you're not busy. *Dog and Duck*. Great nachos there too.

JEN. I'm actually, I'm meeting some friends but thanks.

ALISTAIR. Next time.

ALISTAIR *makes to go*.

Turns back.

I know you

Well, you'll know this already. You've been in the game long enough, but... Do keep seeing your friends. Come to the pub. See your family on the weekends.

Because I know how it can be. It's maybe not what you were expecting. What you were preparing for.

JEN. No, I

It was the same in the police. Similar. I'm used to it.

ALISTAIR. Well we'll see. We need people like you, Jen. We can't afford to lose you. We've lost too many already

,

Stick with it, eh?

JEN. Of, of course, I wasn't

I will do.

ALISTAIR *smiles. Nods.*

ALISTAIR. Night Jen.

JEN. Yea.

Thanks, Alistair.

Night.

Scene Five

Aftermath of dinner at ED *and* NINA*'s.*

MIKE *becomes* ED.

ED, NINA *and* JEN *are sat in the kitchen.*

A fair amount of booze has been drunk.

The atmosphere is light and joyful.

NINA. You sound like a misogynist, Ed.

ED. Unfair. That is unfair. Don't go dropping the 'M' word / on me whenever I criticise a woman.

NINA. / The 'M' word, god's sake. Honestly Jen, she wasn't that bad.

ED. She was entirely inept. She was useless. There were live cables hanging out at one point. And off she went. Five o'clock on the dot. Off she trots, live cables sticking out of the walls.

He mimes checking his watch.

'Ooh, best get home in time for *Pointless*.'

NINA. That's a little unfair.

ED. You're right. Perhaps it is just health and safety gone mad. Might perk the kids up a bit having a current through them. Oscar has been a bit demure of late.

NINA. Oh do shut up, Ed.

JEN. Looks all right now. It's a nice kitchen.

ED. Yes. Because we fired her and got someone else.

NINA. We didn't fire her.

ED (*to* JEN). A man.

No, you're right darling. *I* fired her. Nina wanted to give her another go.

JEN. People deserve second chances, I can see that. She might have had stuff on her mind.

NINA. Thank you, Jen.

ED. Absolutely. I imagine brain surgeons sometimes get a bit distracted thinking about what they're having for tea that night. Get to five o'clock with someone's open skull on their table and think – 'might as well call it a day'.

NINA. Ha ha.

ED. I just don't think it's misogynistic to say that some jobs are done better by men.

NINA. Fuck you!

ED. And women. Some jobs are definitely done better by women. And some by men. It's, it's biology.

NINA. Bullshit.

JEN. Like what?

ED. Eh?

JEN. Like what, what jobs are done better by men and which by women?

ED. Ah, well now you're putting me on the spot.

NINA. Ha! She's got you there.

She grabs JEN *and kisses her on the forehead.*

So great to have you back. I've needed an ally.

JEN *laughs*.

ED. No. Okay, okay. I actually think women make better... doctors.

NINA. What?

ED. See, weren't expecting that one.

NINA. Pulled that out of your arse.

ED. No. No. *Empathy*. Women have a lot more empathy than men. Jen? Right?

JEN. I don't, not my argument Ed.

ED. Well like in your job, surely that's obvious. Men have, there's a reason men, you know, do what they

JEN. Not because of a lack of empathy.

ED. No, no I'm not. I'm not saying that, these guys are monsters

JEN. Well it's not really that either.

ED. Okay, all right, step up to the defence Jen.

JEN. No, I'm not, definitely not defending them, I'm just

Some of them are scarily normal.

NINA. Normal for men.

JEN. Well, yea. You'd go to a callout and they'd be full of fucking poison and rage and then you'd see them in court later and they'd just be sat there in the suit they go to work in every day. Butter wouldn't melt.

ED. Bring back the rack I say. Stretch them till their eyes pop. Stick burning pokers up their arseholes. That's what I'd do, if anyone hurt you my love.

NINA. Very noble of you, darling.

JEN. Well, kind of the point is that it's domestic abuse. So you'd be doing that to yourself.

NINA. Less noble, darling.

ED. Make them watch endless repeats of *Mrs Brown's Boys* until their brain turns to liquid and pours out of their ears.

Have them in that *Black Mirror* episode where

NINA. Jesus Ed, stop getting so excitable. You'll wake up the kids.

(*To* JEN.) Oscar's being a nightmare at the moment. Wakes every two hours through the night like he did when he was a baby. He's seven. We thought those days were long gone.

ED. How wrong we were.

Still, we love them unconditionally, don't we?

NINA. Mm.

ED. I swap between favourites. At the moment it's definitely Lucy.

NINA. Until she threw up in your new shoes.

ED. That was unfortunate. Still, the lack of sleep really has been the deciding factor.

NINA. My lack of sleep you mean.

Ed sleeps like one of those prehistoric people they dig out of bogs centuries later.

ED. It's a skill. What can I say?

NINA. Tit.

Have some cheese. Cheese?

NINA *offers the plate to* JEN.

JEN. Thanks.

NINA. Nothing shuts that man up like cheese.

She smiles at ED.

He is too busy eating to notice.

She shakes her head in despair.

Are you finding this new job okay though, Jen?

JEN. Yea, it's, you know.

It's great.

NINA. ,

Great.

JEN. Yea, it's

Exactly what I

I mean obviously they're all a pain in the arse. Obviously they're all arrogant and belligerent and just bloody… *annoying.*

She laughs.

ED *laughs.*

NINA *looks worried.*

It's like working with children. Really big, dangerous children.

I wanted to clunk their stupid skulls together today. I'm used to dealing with dickheads, but when it's a concentrated group of them and you've got to spend the next however many months trying to strong-arm them into shape...

ED. Shouldn't have given up the day job. At least before you could have whacked them over the head with a truncheon.

NINA. Ed!

ED. Just saying mate, you gave up all the fun bits. Therapy's much less exciting.

JEN. Yea, well. Didn't have much of a choice there, did I?

NINA *gives* ED *a pointed stare.*

He looks embarrassed.

ED. Nah, yea, you're right though. This is much better in the long term.

JEN. Yea.

NINA. And it is, you know

The right thing for you?

JEN. What do you mean?

NINA. Well you know. That this is

JEN. Course.

NINA. Good.

JEN. You don't think?

NINA. No I

,

I just thought, after everything, after you left the police, maybe you'd

Maybe something different.

But

JEN. This is different.

NINA. Yea, but

JEN. It is, Nina. It's fine. I can do it.

NINA. I don't

Of course. I just

ED. Course you can.

(*To* NINA.) Of course she can.

NINA. Yea, sure, of course. It'll be great. You'll be great.

JEN. Yea.

ED. Better hours too, right?

JEN. Exactly, yea. A fair pay cut though. Could be working at Aldi for much the same.

NINA. Oh I love Aldi.

JEN. Tell me about it.

ED. And there we were, hoping you'd be our rich friend.

NINA. *Just rich of heart and mind.*

JEN. And dazzling good looks.

Silence.

NINA. Sorry, I didn't mean

JEN. It's fine.

Really.

NINA. Can't wait to hear more about it.

NINA *smiles at* JEN *warmly.*

JEN *returns it.*

And what about dates? Any good dates recently?

JEN. Not really, no.

ED. Job can't help, can it? Bit of a psychological cock block I imagine.

JEN. Cheers Ed.

NINA. Ignore him!

Ooh, we met this great guy the other week, didn't we?

ED. Who?

NINA. Simon's friend. You know, Dennis.

ED. *Dennis*.

JEN. Christ.

NINA. No, no, maybe like Denny or something. He'd made it cooler.

ED. Not Dennis, *Denton*.

JEN. Much better.

ED *laughs*.

NINA. Well we thought he was great. Didn't we?

ED. My type definitely.

NINA. Shall we set you up?

JEN. Oh god.

NINA. Go on. Can't be worse than strangers on the internet. At least we've vetted him first.

JEN. I mean, that is a point.

NINA. Didn't strike me as a murderer.

ED. Nor me. More the GBH kinda guy. Not all the way.

NINA. Ed, that is so inappropriate. Eat your cheese and shut up.

What do you think, Jen? Up for it?

Scene Six

Community centre room.

The democratic circle.

A few sessions have passed since the first meeting.

MIKE. I'm just saying I've said it before. Numerous times now. And every time you act like it's new information, like I'm hurting your feelings when I say no. And it's actually, like today, like it's actually just really fucking starting to piss me off.

JEN. Let's dig into that then shall we, Mike?

MIKE. With all due respect Jen, that's exactly what we're doing. I'm pissed off and I'm voicing my annoyance. I'm not getting angry. Am I? I'm just voicing that this has irritated me to a degree to which I feel I have to say something. And I'm saying it to the group, aren't I? Not just sharing my annoyance with Frank in a one-to-one capacity

JEN. Yes, and that's really important. But I suppose my question is – why has this annoyed you so much today?

MIKE. Because, oh my god, I've said this before. Haven't I? Or am I completely fucking

I do not want to have to continually bring up that I have a gluten intolerance and therefore can't accept Frank's biscuits which he insists on waving under my nose at every meeting. Tell me I'm wrong, Frank.

FRANK *makes an 'I'm not getting into this' gesture*

Right. And I can't help feeling Jen that this kind of passive-aggressive behaviour is an attempt to make me look like some fucking, some fucking crazy person in front of the rest of the group. And I can't help feeling he's trying to wind me up to stymy my progression because his own is so incredibly deficient.

JEN. Frank. Would you like to say anything?

FRANK. Not particularly.

MIKE. Of course not, Mr Moral High Ground. Just because you're a priest

FRANK. Vicar.

MIKE. Exactly. Just because you're a a

Just because you wear that that fucking

Doesn't mean you're any better than the rest of us. We're all here for the same fucking

JEN. / Mike.

MIKE. / Same fucking

Well, aren't we?

Same fucking indescretions

JEN. Mike.

MIKE. *Offences.*

Aren't we? And if anything, Frank, if anything it makes it *worse* that you're a fucking, dog-collar wearing, high-horsing, upstanding member of the community. At least the rest of us didn't take an oath to be a good fucking, good fucking citizen / of society.

JEN. / Well, now that's interesting, isn't it? Do you not think we all take an oath of some description to be positive members of society,

MIKE *makes to interrupt.*

JEN *raises her hand.*

to respect and care for one another, to make constructive choices that benefit not only yourself but also your fellow man

CHARLIE. And woman.

JEN. Thanks Charlie, yes and woman, to

MIKE. Yea, but

JEN. to be respectful of each other and our differences

MIKE. Yea, but

JEN. Let's open this up to the wider group, shall we? Charlie, what do you think?

CHARLIE *shrugs*.

CHARLIE. Dunno.

MIKE. Charlie hasn't taken fuck, and neither have the rest of us.

JEN. Mike. Warning.

MIKE. I'm just saying, none of us have taken an oath like this guy has. In front of the highest possible power, as he believes it, to say you'll be a good fucking member of society. A god the rest of us, and I don't want to generalise

FRANK. But you're going to.

MIKE. But I'm fucking going to, Frank. *That the rest of us* don't even fucking believe in.

JEN. Maybe not, and let's try not to make assumptions about other people in the group's beliefs shall we? But who else thinks we might have taken, if not a religious oath

FRANK. Commitment.

JEN. Thank you, Frank. Who else thinks that we might have signed up, by being members of the wider society, to some of the same principles that Frank adheres to as part of his Christian faith, or any faith for that matter?

Come on Charlie, what do you think?

Again, MIKE *tries to interrupt*.

Ah, Mike. Please allow Charlie to make a contribution.

CHARLIE. I guess, maybe like at school?

JEN. Okay great, how so?

CHARLIE. Group work and like, maybe PSHE or or

MIKE *snorts*.

JEN. Fantastic, yes. So learning to work alongside each other, and finding out more about our wider society and our place within it, from classes at school.

CHARLIE. Yea.

MIKE. Bollocks.

JEN. Mike.

Brian. Your thoughts.

BRIAN. Yea, I suppose um just generally being part of society is an, there are unspoken rules about what you can and can't

And the law, I guess. We sign up to the law

CHARLIE. Not all of us.

JEN. What's that Charlie?

CHARLIE. Nothing.

BRIAN. Well, yea, suppose Charlie's right. We're here because we didn't, chose not to to

Yea, all broke the law I guess.

JEN. The law, yes. But what else?

CHARLIE. Morals. Being a good person. Generally just not

You know.

JEN. Right. Yes, good. Anyone else? Frank? What does the Bible say?

MIKE. The Bible says you can stone your wife to death for adultery.

JEN. Mike. I am going to ask you to leave in a minute. This is a group session. Please listen to what other people have to say.

MIKE. Just saying.

JEN. Frank. Your thoughts please.

FRANK. Well, yes, so I choose to live my life in line with the teachings of our Lord.

MIKE (*mutters*). Not my Lord.

FRANK. My life has been committed to following the word of God and encouraging others to follow suit. I have been, at times, far from perfect

MIKE. Hmh!

FRANK. but I seek to better myself with each passing day. I recognise each struggle I have faced as a test from God.

MIKE. And how would you say you've done in those tests, mate?

JEN. Thank you, Mike. Perhaps I can suggest we raise hands if we'd like to comment.

FRANK. It is a fair question. And it's something I do ask myself regularly.

MIKE. And?

JEN looks at MIKE pointedly.

He puts up his hand.

JEN. Mike?

MIKE. *And?*

FRANK. And I'm aware that I haven't been entirely successful at passing those tests with the grace and dignity expected of me.

MIKE (*to* BRIAN). Well that's one way to describe forty years of knocking your missus about.

JEN. So what are some of the social rules we follow in this country? Brian?

BRIAN. What like, um no murdering?

JEN. Yes.

BRIAN. No stealing, no rape, no um tax avoidance.

MIKE. All right, Moses.

JEN. Okay great, yes. So those are some of the topline ones

MIKE. Tax avoidance?

CHARLIE. Yea, my uncle went to prison for ages for that. Tried to put a load of money offshore, but turns out his accountant was having him on.

MIKE. Eh?

JEN. Back on topic, please. So those are some of the more serious crimes you can commit, but what about the morals we adhere to on a day to day basis. Mike?

MIKE. God knows.

JEN. Charlie?

CHARLIE. Be respectful to your mum.

JEN. Respect. Great.

CHARLIE. Say please and thank you.

JEN. Politeness. Good.

,

Any more?

,

How about treating others how you would want to be treated yourself? Being kind and generous to other people.

FRANK. Jealousy – of what other people have. Coveting your neighbour's goods.

JEN. Excellent. And what about how we extend this into our relationships? Should we be jealous of our partners? How can we ensure that we are treating them with respect and dignity? How can we make sure we're equals, that there isn't a power imbalance in the relationship?

MIKE. Well yea but that's bollocks, isn't it?

JEN. How's that?

MIKE. It's so one sided. Women harp on about equality, but you also want to be looked after and have stuff paid for by us, but also for us to do the dishwasher and take out the bins and put up the shelves

BRIAN. Yea.

MIKE. Everyone's shitting all over men these days. Can't bloody win. Can't say anything any more and god help you if you try and make a joke.

JEN. I don't think that's strictly

BRIAN. Can't be left alone in a room with a woman cos you never know what she might to accuse you of

JEN. Hang on

BRIAN. Become an absolute witchhunt. All they have to do is point the finger, and that's it. *Cancelled*.

MIKE. Yea, *cancelled*!

JEN. Well, I don't think that's actually true. Do you know the number of rape cases where the perpetrator is / actually prosecuted?

BRIAN. / Someone always saying they've been assaulted nowadays.

CHARLIE. My mate got accused of it, few months back. Had the police at his door.

JEN. Yes, maybe that's because

CHARLIE. His mum chucked him out of the house. No proof neither.

JEN. Look, can we get back on topic please? This is / spiralling.

BRIAN. / Women are always saying how hard it is for them. Well what about us? No one cares about what it's like to be a man any more.

MIKE. If in doubt, blame the guy.

BRIAN. Yea. We're always the villain.

MIKE. Always the bad guy. Take the blame for all the world's problems these days.

BRIAN. Even when you've done nothing wrong.

JEN. Nothing wrong?!

You beat your fucking partners to a pulp!

,

Silence.

JEN *breathes hard.*

The room is tense.

Sorry.

That wasn't

,

Sorry.

,

Let's move on.

Shall we?

Scene Seven

The centre.

Hallway.

JEN *stands, leaning against the wall.*

Psyching herself up for the session ahead.

NINA *becomes* BELINDA.

BELINDA *approaches holding a tin of scones.*

BELINDA. You're new here, aren't you?

JEN. Oh. Hello. Um…

BELINDA. Belinda.

,

Frank's wife?

JEN. Of course, lovely to meet you. I'm Jen.

BELINDA. I know. Frank told me.

JEN. Oh?

BELINDA. I hope they're treating you well, those boys. Frank says they can be hard work sometimes, but they've got good enough hearts.

JEN. Did he?

BELINDA. I made you all some scones. I like to give something to Frank to bring in each week.

JEN. That's very nice of you.

BELINDA. Well. I used to do it for the boys when they were in school. Nice way for you to meet people I always think, having something to offer. Doesn't take much, but it means a lot to people, doesn't it?

JEN. Absolutely.

BELINDA. So, you're settling in okay?

JEN. Um, yes. Thank you.

BELINDA. Good. Nice place here. Everyone's so sweet and helpful. Is Alistair looking after you?

JEN. Er, yes.

BELINDA. Oh lovely. He's lovely. Been here a long time, I think, Alistair. He's probably told you. Told me he'd been here twenty-seven years.

JEN. I think so, yes.

BELINDA. Twenty-seven years! Such a long time for a young man. Do you like scones, Jen?

JEN. Er, yes.

BELINDA. Good. Frank loves scones. Can't get enough. I have to be careful with him. He'd eat the lot if he could. That's why I get him to bring them here. Otherwise they sit at home and we eat them. I'm just as bad. No self-control. I'd eat twenty-four-seven if I could. Couldn't you? No self-control. I came here a while back to that Weight Watchers. WW now, isn't it? As if they think we don't still know what it stands for. I lost three and a half stone. Put it straight back on of course. But I was pleased with myself for that.

JEN. Yes, that's

BELINDA. I was pleased. Could fit into some of my old dresses again. Frank said for years 'Why do you keep all these dresses when they don't fit?' And I always said maybe one

day they would. And they did! For a short while anyway.
I am naughty. Straight back on. You wouldn't believe how
long it took me to lose that weight, and then it was back on
again in the blink of an eye. No self-control.

Anyway.

Blabbermouth.

Would you give these to Frank for me?

She indicates the scones.

I left them in the car like an idiot so I said I'd go back for
them so he could go in ahead. But now I've seen you, you
could give them to him for me, couldn't you?

JEN. Absolutely.

BELINDA *presses the tin into* JEN*'s hands.*

JEN *takes the tin, but* BELINDA *doesn't let go.*

BELINDA. He's a good man, Frank.

JEN. Right.

BELINDA. I know you, well you might think a lot of things.
But he loves me very dearly, and I do too.

JEN. Okay.

BELINDA. He's had a difficult time over the years.

ALISTAIR *enters.*

BELINDA *lets go of the tin.*

A smile returns to her face.

Thanks Jen.

Oh, speak of the devil.

ALISTAIR *stops by them.*

ALISTAIR. Hello Belinda.

BELINDA. I've just met Jen.

ALISTAIR. So I see. How are you keeping?

BELINDA. Oh well, well. Scones today Alistair.

ALISTAIR. Delicious. Thank you.

BELINDA. Alistair loves my scones.

JEN. Does he?

ALISTAIR. Not as much as your millionaire shortbread.

BELINDA. Oh gosh yes. Those did go down well. I'll have to do them again another week.

ALISTAIR. Only if you've got time, Belinda.

BELINDA. Time is all I have, Alistair. I'd best be off, let you get on. I'll be back at the end of the evening. Nice to meet you, Jen. Alistair.

JEN. And you.

ALISTAIR. Thanks Belinda.

BELINDA exits.

There is a pause to ensure she has definitely left.

ALISTAIR *smiles at* JEN.

She's great.

JEN. Yes. Yea, she's

That was

Surreal.

ALISTAIR. She's very supportive of Frank's 'recovery'. Her word.

He's what we call a 'regular'.

JEN. Right.

It's just

ALISTAIR. Yes.

JEN. In his notes it says he broke her jaw.

ALISTAIR. Yes.

JEN. She needed an operation to fix it.

ALISTAIR. He's done a lot worse than that over the years. That was just the thing he got done for.

Don't let me hold you up.

ALISTAIR *indicates for* JEN *to go in*.

JEN *pauses for a moment*.

Then enters the session room.

Scene Eight

Bar.

JEN *and* NINA *sit on velvet-covered stools*.

They are a few drinks in.

JEN. Godddd. Awful.

NINA. Sorry.

JEN. He was *awful*. You can't make these people up.

NINA. Sorry.

JEN. I thought

I don't know.

After Sam I thought

NINA. I know.

JEN. I thought, I'll easily meet someone.

NINA. Yea.

JEN. There's loads of great, single guys out there waiting to be met.

NINA. Yea.

JEN. It's been four years. Nearly five.

NINA. Sorry hun.

JEN. And now I look back on that time with Sam and I think, was it even that great? He used to talk over me all the time and took zero interest in my work.

NINA. Yea, he was a prick.

JEN. Was he?

NINA. One of the nicer pricks.

JEN. Jesus. And then tonight. Gooddd. I thought I'd seen the worst of them, but this guy

NINA. He seemed so great when we met him.

JEN. Maybe because he didn't want to shag you. Or maybe he did and didn't want to shag me. Men seem to have different personalities depending on whether they want to shag you or not.

NINA. In fairness, I have a different personality when I want to shag someone too. I think it's just such a surprise when you meet someone shaggable.

JEN. Tell me about it.

NINA. Was Dennis not at least shaggable?

JEN. Oh entirely.

NINA. Well

JEN. Until he opened his mouth.

NINA. Gotcha.

JEN. Very hard to see past that.

NINA. They do exist.

JEN. I know.

NINA. There are good men around.

JEN. I know.

Probably all married though, aren't they?

NINA. Probably. Though even then…

JEN. Ed's all right, isn't he?

NINA. Mostly. Yes, no I'm being unfair. Most of the time he's fine. Great even. Just sometimes

JEN. Yea.

NINA. sometimes I want to castrate him. Smug prick.

PETER enters.

He looks around the bar.

Sees JEN *and* NINA.

They don't see him.

Some of the things he comes out with. He's on his high horse at the moment about that children's TV presenter. 'When will it end?' he keeps saying. Not, 'When will they stop shagging underage girls?' It's, 'When will they stop this witchhunt?'

JEN. Children.

NINA. Sorry?

JEN. Underage girls are

Doesn't matter.

Yea mate, that sounds insufferable.

PETER approaches them.

PETER. Hello.

JEN. Hello?

PETER. You're back.

JEN. Oh, um, yea.

PETER. Your local, is it?

JEN. Not exactly.

NINA. It's mine. We're here all the time.

PETER. Oh really?

Pause.

JEN *shoots* NINA *a look.*

PETER *looks expectantly at* JEN *to introduce him to* NINA. *She doesn't.*

I'm Peter.

NINA. Peter. I'm Nina.

PETER. Nice to meet you.

NINA. How do you two

JEN. / We don't really.

PETER. / We dated for a bit.

JEN. Once. We went on one date. Couple of weeks back.

PETER. Here, actually.

JEN. Yea.

PETER. Didn't get back to me, did she?

NINA. She's a heartbreaker, our Jen.

JEN. I've been busy.

PETER. Oh yea no I get it. Me too. I'm just teasing.

NINA. So. What is it you do, Peter?

JEN. Nina.

NINA. What?

PETER. I work for a housing developer. Working on that plot down by Gatacre Lane.

NINA. Oh yea. I know it.

PETER. Yea, load of luxury apartments.

NINA. Wow.

PETER. Yea, they'll be pretty impressive once they're up.

NINA. Nice.

(*To* JEN.) Nice.

Pause.

PETER. Can I get you ladies a drink?

JEN. No thanks.

NINA. Oh, um

Looks to JEN.

No thanks, Peter. That's very kind.

PETER. Well nice to meet you, Nina. Nice to see you Jen. Let me know if

JEN. Yea.

PETER. Enjoy your evening.

NINA. And you.

JEN. Yup. You too.

PETER *walks away.*

NINA. Oh he was nice.

JEN. Yea.

NINA. You should go out with him again.

JEN. Bit weird he's here, no?

NINA. Why? Maybe it's his local too.

JEN. I don't think so. I'm sure he got the train last time. Lives in Chelmsford or somewhere.

NINA. Well then he must have put a tracker on your phone and followed you here.

JEN. Shut up.

,

Who's he here with?

NINA. Maybe another date.

JEN. Didn't look like it.

NINA. Jealous?

JEN. No.

NINA. You should be. He's cute.

JEN. You can't pull off 'cute'. Only Americans say 'cute'.

NINA. Well then he's *hot*. Hot like a McDonald's apple pie.

JEN. Everything I'm looking for!

NINA. Let's wife swap. You can have Ed. I'll have Peter the *hunk*.

JEN. Such a hunk.

NINA. Such a hunk.

JEN. ,

Still think it's weird he's here.

NINA. Oh stop. Ed was right, your job's making you paranoid.

JEN. Maybe.

NINA. See him again. I think it's fate. You can't ignore fate.

JEN *scoffs*.

What?

JEN. I wish reality was as nice as the way it seems in your head.

NINA. Oh shut your face.

Scene Nine

The centre.

The democratic circle set up again.

The mood is lighter today.

The men more comfortable with each other.

BRIAN. Maybe yoga, or or, taekwondo or something.

JEN. Great suggestion.

FRANK. I find prayer is very helpful.

BRIAN. Meditation.

JEN. Right. Good. Anything else? Charlie?

CHARLIE. Gymnastics?

MIKE *laughs*.

MIKE. *Gymnastics?*

CHARLIE. No, not

What do I mean?

MIKE. Not gymnastics, mate.

JEN. Okay. We know what you mean though, Charlie.

MIKE. Do we?

JEN. Why don't you tell us what you meant, Charlie?

CHARLIE. I dunno. You know, like like the bendy one. Like what Brian said.

FRANK. Yoga?

CHARLIE. Yea, but like the other one.

MIKE. *The other one.*

BRIAN. Pilates?

CHARLIE. Yea. My mum used to do it.

MIKE. Hilarious.

BRIAN. My missus did it too.

CHARLIE. Yea. She said it helped her concentrate. Cos it was hard, y'know. Focus on her body or or like the movements or something.

BRIAN. Yea, my missus said the same. Calmed her down. Endorphins and stuff.

JEN. Well that's

BRIAN. Did it for about a year but then I broke her arm and she couldn't do it again. Didn't heal properly.

MIKE. Fucking hell.

JEN. Okay, Brian. Thanks, thanks for that.

What other tactics could we employ? Any other suggestions?

FRANK. I find a long walk is helpful. Clears the mind.

JEN. Right. Good, that's really good. Okay so

MIKE. Sorry. Sorry, just to play devil's advocate

The group collectively groans.

No, no, I just

I'm just trying to understand how this will help in the heat of the moment. So, okay, so someone pisses you off Brian, yea? And your suggestion is to, what, do some pilates?

BRIAN. No

MIKE. Cos that's sort of what you're saying, mate. You're saying someone's really pushing your fucking buttons and you're going to go into downward dog.

CHARLIE. That's yoga.

MIKE. Same difference.

JEN. Okay

MIKE. No, I'm not, I'm not being pedantic

The group audibly disagree with this statement.

I'm just saying it's not practical. Is it? Well is it?

JEN. It's not about in the heat of the moment, Mike. It's about finding tactics in general to

MIKE. Well how's that going / to help

JEN. / in the long run to help calm, help you channel / your emotions

MIKE. / *channel my emotions*. Most people take cocaine or drink whiskey for that, Jen.

JEN. Yes well

MIKE. You should try that maybe, help you lighten up a bit.

JEN. Thank you.

PART ONE, SCENE NINE 51

MIKE. I'm not, I'm just saying there are other ways.

JEN. Yes, but these ways are much less destructive.

BRIAN. I like Lego. I was building my Millennium Falcon for a while and that helped me calm down.

JEN. That's great.

BRIAN. Although I realised the other week that one of the pieces wasn't in the box. And I looked and looked but it wasn't there. I thought maybe one of the kids had taken it with them when their mum

And it was a really key piece to finishing it all off and I got so angry I smashed the whole thing up. And then I found the piece under the sofa a few days later so I've started again.

Pause.

MIKE. Well at least you've spun it out a bit longer, Bri.

JEN. Yes, okay. Well what could you have done instead of smashing it up, Brian?

MIKE. Could have done some yoga.

BRIAN. Oh fuck off, Mike.

MIKE. Just saying.

JEN. Brian?

No?

Frank, Charlie? Any thoughts?

FRANK. Perhaps some breathing. Take himself away from the problem for a moment. Reassess the situation.

JEN. Great.

MIKE. That's what you'd do, is it Frank?

JEN. I think that's a great suggestion.

Okay, so let's split up into groups. I want you to take it in turns to tell your partner about a time when you were really angry about something and what you did in that situation. Then I want you to come up with ways you could have acted differently, and what you might do going forwards if that same situation happened again. Like Brian's example just now.

BRIAN. I've found all the pieces now. I've got them labelled.

JEN. Yes, okay well *hypothetically*

BRIAN. Yea, but I mean it won't happen again because I've

JEN. Then a different example, Brian. I imagine you've got other examples of times you've been angry.

MIKE. Eh, eh. Pass-ag or what?

JEN. Mike and Charlie make a pair. Frank and Brian.

MIKE. Delighted. Come on Chaz, I'll show you my Full Moon.

The men move off into their separate groups.

MIKE *turns back and winks at* JEN.

She can't help but laugh.

JEN. God's sake.

MIKE *grins*.

A moment between them.

Taking advantage of the lighter mood, JEN *puts on some music.*

The men are relaxed, chatty.

MIKE *is upside down in a ridiculous yoga position.*

The others stop to watch him, laughing.

JEN *is looser, her guard down for a moment.*

SIOBHAN *enters.*

She watches them all for a moment in disgust.

Looks around the room, spots BRIAN.

SIOBHAN. You. You piece of utter shit.

She charges up to him.

MIKE. Whoa.

JEN. Oh god.

JEN freezes.

The men all stop what they're doing to look at SIOBHAN.

SIOBHAN. You utter fucking shitbag.

FRANK (*to* SIOBHAN). Sorry. I don't think you're allowed in here.

(*To* JEN.) She's not allowed in here, / is she?

SIOBHAN (*to* JEN). You running this, are you?

JEN looks at her, frozen to the spot.

You know what he's been doing?

BRIAN. Siobhan.

SIOBHAN. Don't *Siobhan* me you little turd.

MIKE *laughs*.

MIKE. Brilliant.

SIOBHAN (*to* JEN). He's been coming to the school. Turning up at their lunch breaks and talking to them through the fence. Trying to take them

BRIAN. Not trying to take them, Siobhan. Trying to *talk* to them.

SIOBHAN. Not what they say, Brian. Not what my kids are saying. 'Don't tell Mummy,' you've been saying. 'Don't tell Mummy because Brian will get in trouble.' Well guess what Brian, you're in fucking trouble now. Trying to steal my fucking kids? Well you know what, Bri, I will make sure you *never* see those kids again. You hear? Never.

BRIAN. Fuck you.

FRANK. Whoa, come on now Brian.

BRIAN. And fuck you, Frank. Fuck all of you.

SIOBHAN. See what he's like. See?

MIKE. All right, just, maybe calm down, okay?

Jen?

JEN. I

MIKE. Jen? Fucking hell.

JEN. / I, I

She seems to snap out of it slightly.

Yes. Charlie, can you... the music?

CHARLIE. Okay.

JEN. And Mike, you, can you go and get one of the other staff?

MIKE. What?

JEN. Now. Please.

MIKE looks at JEN quizzically, but exits.

CHARLIE turns off the music.

SIOBHAN. You've had it you little shit. Never again.

BRIAN advances on her.

Dangerous.

CHARLIE and FRANK rush to grab him.

FRANK. Come on now, Brian, you'll make things a hundred times worse for yourself.

SIOBHAN. Yea, that's right. Stick up for him. You're all here for the same reason I guess? You wife-beating pricks. You told them what you did to me, Brian? Have you? Nine weeks, he got. Nine fucking weeks. And now I'm homeless, having to beg off the state. And he's here getting free fucking therapy.

JEN. Siobhan, you can't be here. Please, please just leave.

SIOBHAN. I'm going, going. Can't stand to be round any of you.

I'll get you for this, Brian. You mark my words. I will get you for this.

JEN. Siobhan

SIOBHAN (*to* JEN). You're worse than the lot of them. Fucking traitor.

JEN. Siobhan.

SIOBHAN. I'm gone.

She turns.

BRIAN *lets out a roar.*

SIOBHAN *stops at the door and looks him square in the eyes.*

Then exits.

BRIAN *cries out again,* CHARLIE *and* FRANK *still holding him.*

JEN *is shaking.*

PART TWO

Scene One

A bowling alley.

JEN *and* PETER *take turns at the lane.*

A small table with a couple of drinks between them.

JEN*'s is nearly all gone.*

PETER *bowls.*

PETER. Strike!

He celebrates.

JEN *steps up to take her place.*

Doesn't acknowledge his success.

I didn't think I'd see you again actually.

JEN. Me neither if I'm honest.

PETER. Oh.

JEN. I mean

Sorry. I mean

She bowls.

Watches the ball.

My friends tell me I'm too quick to judge. To write people off.

She looks disappointed with her bowl.

PETER. Ahh bad luck.

Are they right? Your friends.

JEN. Probably.

PETER *walks forwards with the ball.*

Holds it up.

Measures the shot with a 'professional' eye.

Bowls.

PETER. Yes mate!

JEN. Nice one.

JEN *steps forwards with the ball.*

PETER *comes up behind her.*

He holds her from behind.

JEN *tenses.*

PETER. You want to line the centre up with the ball. Then take a decisive swing.

JEN *goes to swing.*

Whoa careful. Death by bowling ball.

JEN *bowls again.*

It slips into the gutters.

JEN. Fuck's sake.

PETER. You want to

JEN. I think I might just have a break for a bit.

PETER. We're nearly through. We could just

JEN. I'm just going to take a break for a bit.

PETER. Sure, okay.

Mind if I

JEN. Knock yourself out.

PETER *steps forwards to bowl.*

He continues to bowl both his and JEN*'s turns.*

Tries not to look too pleased with himself.

PETER. Apologies it's so dead in here.

JEN. That's okay.

PETER. I guess most people don't go bowling quite so late.

JEN. Oh, sorry, yea. Work is

PETER. That's okay. I'm glad we could see each other again.

JEN. Yea.

PETER. Nice to do an activity. Good for bonding.

JEN. Yea.

PETER. I'm a bit of a bowling freak actually. Love it. Used to be on a team.

JEN. Oh wow.

PETER. Only fun. Just something me and my home mates used to do.

Then, well

Everyone just drifts off in different directions don't they?

JEN. You could start up another one?

PETER. Ahh everyone's really spread out these days.

JEN. I meant with your new friends.

PETER. Er, yea.

,

JEN. Or with new people?

PETER. Yea.

Yea, I mean. With work. I don't really have time for friends as much these days.

JEN. What, not at all?

PETER. Well, yea, I mean, I've *got friends.*

JEN. Sure.

PETER. But like, lots of them are shacked up and
   Well.

   No one's got any spare time at our age, do they?

JEN. I don't know what I'd do without my friends.

PETER. Yea well it's different for girls, isn't it?

JEN. Is it?

PETER. Yea. Men are just better at being on their own.

   Girls like to, you know

JEN. Natter?

PETER. You know what I mean.

JEN. I dunno. I guess maybe women are just good at supporting each other. Not just relying on their partners for everything.

PETER. Yea, but like in *proper* relationships that's not right.

JEN. ,

   What do you mean?

PETER. Well like my mum and dad only really have each other and they've got a great relationship. They don't need anyone else.

   JEN *nods slowly.*

JEN. Sure.

   PETER *looks embarrassed.*

   He bowls fiercely.

   It goes off course and ends up in the gutter.

PETER. Ah fuck.

JEN. ,

   I guess maybe some people are lucky like that.

   She stands.

Walks towards him, conciliatory.

So go on, what's your top bowling tip?

PETER. Um. Well, you've got to make sure you're not swinging the ball back at an angle. You want it to go as straight as possible. So get the initial angle of release right, with the right amount of force, and you're onto a winner.

JEN. Okay.

PETER. Cos before you were

He demonstrates.

JEN. Gotcha.

PETER. Give it a go.

JEN makes an attempt.

PETER guides her.

She bowls.

It is obviously another pretty crap bowl.

JEN. Ah for god's

PETER. Hey, one is better than none.

JEN. Thanks Peter.

PETER's mood has evidently improved.

PETER. Well I got your score up a bit, so we're not too far apart now.

JEN. Cheers, yea.

JEN goes back to the table.

Drains her drink.

PETER joins her.

PETER. Did I tell you they've given me a promotion? At work.

JEN. Since we last

PETER. Yea.

JEN. Wow. Congratulations.

PETER. Yea, I mean it's great but it's not a big deal. I've had a few over the years.

JEN. Right. Well I guess you've been there so long.

PETER. Sorry?

JEN. You know, because you've been there so long I guess

PETER. They promote me because I'm really good at what I do.

JEN. No, sure.

PETER. I helped us win the Regional Best Older People's Housing Development Award for 2017.

JEN. Did

Wow. That's impressive.

PETER. Yea it's, whatever. It was a while ago.

JEN. Sure.

Still though, that's

PETER. Thanks.

Yea, I guess it was pretty competitive.

How about you though?

JEN. I don't think they give awards out for my job.

PETER. No I meant like, what's the trajectory with your role?

JEN. Oh, um, mostly to the pub.

,

No, I'm being

It's yea, I mean it's

Well it's pretty fucking exhausting to be honest.

PETER. Right.

JEN. Not sure what I was thinking.

I thought maybe this would be

You know. Easier or

I dunno.

At least maybe better than being a PC. Just turning up after something's already happened, you know? Getting in first, before anything does go wrong. Changing these people from the inside out.

PETER. Sure.

JEN. But now I'm just scared of making the wrong

,

Another wrong

,

Cos I worked with this woman, right, Gloria. Before. When I was a

I didn't work *with* her. Not like that. She was more, well a regular I guess. We'd get called out to her constantly. Always the same thing. He'd gone out, got pissed, come home and beaten her up. And the neighbours were always calling us up. Worried about her at first, you know. But then I think just annoyed at the noise.

And every time it was the same. 'No, no, nothing's wrong. Don't come in. I'm fine. We're just playing. It's the dog. It's the telly. We'll turn it down. Won't be so loud. Sorry for the disturbance. Won't happen again.'

And of course it did.

Time and time again. Always the same call. Always the same response. But she wouldn't fucking leave him. Wouldn't press charges. Couldn't even conceive of the idea. 'He doesn't mean it. He's just messing around. He loves me. He worships me. Wouldn't hurt a hair on my head.'

And then one day he killed her and I had a breakdown and had to leave the force.

She laughs.

Silence.

Not a proper

Not an actual breakdown.

Silence.

PETER. Wanna finish up and go back to mine? I've got this really nice red on the go. An Argentinian Malbec?

JEN. ,

Sure.

Why not?

Scene Two

Alistair's office.

JEN *enters.*

ALISTAIR *is eating from a Tupperware.*

ALISTAIR. Jen. Take a seat.

JEN. Thanks.

ALISTAIR. Don't mind me eating while we chat, do you?

JEN. Er no, not at

ALISTAIR. Haven't quite managed to find time to take a break today. Or for the last twenty years for that matter.

JEN. Sure.

ALISTAIR. My husband's got me on this, I don't know, some kind of diet. Says we're both putting on weight like crazy. He thinks something's wrong. Thyroid, he says. As if we'd both, at the same time, you know? I hate to break it to him that it's just being over fifty. Wish he'd just buy himself a sports car. At least then I wouldn't have to partake in his midlife crisis. I have dreams he's a walking, talking doughnut most nights.

JEN *laughs politely.*

ALISTAIR *does not.*

Mm, so talk to me.

JEN. Erm

ALISTAIR. How are you getting on? All right?

JEN. Oh, yea, great yea.

ALISTAIR. Any better since you asked, who was it, Brian to leave the programme?

JEN. Yea. I mean. Of course. It was the right thing to do. Right?

ALISTAIR. Right.

JEN. He couldn't have stayed. I mean what kind of message would that have

To the others.

ALISTAIR. Quite. Although I do always think people benefit much more from being here than, well, *not* being here.

JEN. Right. Yea but

He broke the terms of his restraining order.

ALISTAIR. Absolutely.

JEN. And the others would

I have to think about the others in all of this.

ALISTAIR. Quite right.

JEN. Right, yea. So. And I mean they're definitely, definitely starting to

Starting to open up.

ALISTAIR. Great.

JEN. It's taken a while, obviously.

I mean they're… you know. They're not easy.

ALISTAIR. Of course not.

JEN. Yea.

And they're, sometimes I feel like we're going round in circles a bit

ALISTAIR. Right.

JEN. and that they're, they're not necessarily responding the way I would

ALISTAIR. Right.

JEN. you know, how I would have hoped, after this amount of time.

ALISTAIR. I see.

JEN. You know, I thought perhaps by this point

ALISTAIR. Jen. I'm going to stop you there. There's a lot of pressure in jobs like these to 'fix' the entire problem, otherwise you feel like you've failed in some way. We're only a tiny piece of the puzzle. It just might be that for some of these men we're the final bit.

For others...

He raises his hands.

'Who knows?'

JEN. Right, yea. And I know that, I do. I just

It's just

Funding's so tight, do you ever wonder if it would be better to put it into refuges? Rather than

You know.

ALISTAIR. Domestic abuse is endemic. You can't just chop back a few ugly stragglers. You've got to attack it at the root. It'll keep coming back and back unless you get it at the base.

That's what we're doing.

One group at a time.

JEN. I mean it's why I left the Met. Couldn't bear it playing out time and time again with nothing changing. So I thought

Here.

I thought maybe I could

But I

ALISTAIR. You're doing something good here, Jen. Not everyone can say that. I've been impressed by what I've seen in your supervised sessions. You're getting them to open up in ways they probably never have before.

JEN. Thanks, yea, it's just

ALISTAIR. Keep going. Keep pushing them. You might be surprised.

JEN. Yup. Yea, okay thanks.

ALISTAIR. Oh just to let you know the Thursday evening Positive Parenting sessions are going to be cut from next month because yet another grant has fallen through.

JEN. Okay, um. Fine.

ALISTAIR. And I spoke to your old Superintendent.

JEN. ,

Oh.

Oh, what did he

ALISTAIR. Just rang the other day. Asking after you. How you were getting on.

JEN. Right.

ALISTAIR. I said you were doing great.

JEN. Oh.

,

Thanks.

ALISTAIR. He said you're one to hang on to. We're lucky to have you. I said I know.

JEN. Did he say

ALISTAIR. Nothing else. Just that really. Just thought you should know.

He smiles.

JEN *hesitates. Completely thrown.*

JEN. Um

ALISTAIR. Well then, if that's all? I'll be honest, these lentils are wreaking havoc with my inner workings so I'd suggest you don't hang around too much longer.

JEN. Oh. Yes, absolutely.

Thanks, Alistair.

JEN *makes to go.*

Then stops. Turns around.

I am

I'm fine now. After the

After I

,

I'm not

ALISTAIR. I know.

He smiles again. Nods.

She nods. Heart in her mouth.

Then leaves.

Scene Three

The group.

CHARLIE, MIKE, *and* FRANK *bring in chairs and the same circle is formed.*

CHARLIE. Thursdays, curry night. Curry and a pint for a fiver. Go at five thirty, home by ten. Beat my mum up for a while. Bed by ten thirty.

Which was fine.

But then the pub started doing fish and chip night on Wednesdays. And pie and pint nights Mondays. And Fridays were karaoke and he loved that.

And then it was four times a week.

Just needed to get it out somehow, I guess.

And she was there. Always there.

Cos otherwise we were there. And she didn't want that.

He shrugs.

So. Yea.

JEN. Thanks Charlie.

CHARLIE. Not a fucking sob story. You asked.

JEN. I did.

CHARLIE. And I don't hate him. I know you think I should.

JEN. I don't think anything.

CHARLIE. Well I don't. He had a hard job and a hard childhood. And my mum could be a pain in the arse. Us too I guess. And he was

FRANK. And that made it okay for him to hit you?

MIKE. Oh shut up, Frank.

FRANK. I'm just saying.

JEN. Mike. Frank.

CHARLIE. No. Not saying that. Just saying

Doesn't matter.

JEN. No, go on. What did you want to say Charlie?

CHARLIE. Nothing. Doesn't matter.

JEN. I think it would be really helpful if you could try.

CHARLIE. No, cos Frank's all up in my face now.

MIKE. Yea.

FRANK. What, no I'm

JEN. Charlie, no one's judging you. What were you going to say?

MIKE. Frank is. Judging everyone from up there on his, his fucking

Acting like he hasn't been knocking his missus around for

JEN. Mike.

MIKE. for the last forty

FRANK. We're not on me, okay? We're talking about Charlie.

MIKE. Too fucking right we are, Frank.

JEN. Both of you. Just settle okay?

Charlie. What were you trying to say?

CHARLIE. Nothing, it doesn't matter.

MIKE. That's you, that is Frank.

FRANK. I asked a perfectly legitimate question, something maybe he hadn't thought about himself.

MIKE. Legitimate? Not your job mate. Might have been once, you hypocrite, / but now

JEN. / All right.

That's enough.

I know things have been a little unsettled in recent

Since Brian left the group.

But let's try to all

Just

Shh, okay?

MIKE. I don't think you're meant to tell us to shut up, Jen.

JEN. I didn't.

MIKE. This is a safe space where we're meant to be allowed to share our innermost

JEN. Yes.

MIKE. And *shh*-ing us isn't going to help.

JEN. I know, and I apologise.

MIKE *sits back in his chair, triumphant.*

Right

CHARLIE. I tried texting him, but he hasn't texted back.

JEN. Who, Charlie?

CHARLIE. Brian.

JEN. Okay, well, technically you're not really supposed to have each other's / numbers but

CHARLIE. / Said he'd give me a recipe for banana bread. Got some old bananas at home. Won't last much longer though.

MIKE. Look it up. BBC Good Food.

CHARLIE. Could do yea.

MIKE. Man, I miss banana bread.

FRANK. There'll be a gluten-free recipe for that online.

MIKE. Butt out, Frank.

JEN. Well, there's a lot going on for Brian at the moment. He's committed a very serious offence.

MIKE. Allegedly.

JEN. Yes, allegedly.

MIKE. Innocent until proven guilty.

JEN. Yes.

MIKE. Shouldn't have thrown him out before it was a hundred per cent. That's discrimination.

JEN. Uh huh.

MIKE. Like me. Never proven.

FRANK. Yet.

MIKE. What d'you say, Frank?

JEN. Cool it.

Frank, why don't you tell us how your week has been?

FRANK. Fine, yes, thank you.

JEN. Any moments of

Where you've lost control?

FRANK. No.

JEN. No?

FRANK. Belinda put us on a diet this week.

JEN. Okay. How was that?

FRANK. Fine.

JEN. Because sometimes a restricted diet can make us more

FRANK. It was fine. I feel better in general. More vegetables can do that.

JEN. Okay. Good. And what about exercise? Have you found something that helps relieve tension?

FRANK. No.

JEN. Okay.

FRANK. I don't need exercise when I have prayer.

MIKE. In fairness Frank, you had prayer before and you still beat up your wife.

JEN. Oh for god's

FRANK. What is it about me that riles you so much Mike? Let's drill into that shall we?

JEN. I'm not sure that's a good idea.

CHARLIE. It does seem like you've got it in for him, Mike.

MIKE. Not especially.

CHARLIE. I'd say so.

MIKE. I've got it in for all of you. Frank's just the most hypocritical. I can't stand a hypocrite.

FRANK. And you're not?

MIKE. Not like you, Frank.

CHARLIE (*almost inaudible*). We're all fucking hypocrites, aren't we?

JEN. What was that, Charlie?

FRANK. At least I've owned up to my mistakes, / what have you done towards owning up to

MIKE. / Oh your 'mistakes'. Your *mistakes* have been

And I *have* owned up to what I've done in the past but this last case against me has never been proved. Never proved.

FRANK. God will be / your judge.

MIKE. / Fuck your God.

JEN. Enough!

Charlie. What were you saying?

CHARLIE. I said we're all hypocrites. Sometimes I wanted him to hit her. Sometimes I wanted to punch her in the fucking face myself for being such a spineless piece of shit. She could have taken us out of that years before but she didn't. She didn't and now she's dead and he's in prison and I'm here and I've got a baby coming who I'll never meet probably and instead I'm stuck here listening to your endless bullshit.

,

(*To* JEN.) Happy now?

Pause.

JEN. Do you understand why she didn't take you out of that situation, Charlie?

CHARLIE. No.

JEN. If you had to guess. Put yourself in her shoes.

CHARLIE. Cos she was scared.

JEN. Yes.

CHARLIE. Cos she had no money and her family were all in Scotland and she was down here and she hadn't spoken to them for years because of him, because he was really controlling of who she spoke to and when and eventually they all just gave up trying.

JEN. Right.

CHARLIE. She was still a fucking bitch though.

He starts to cry.

FRANK. Thank you for sharing, Charlie.

JEN. Yes, thank you, Charlie.

MIKE. Yup.

JEN. So do you have a partner at the moment?

CHARLIE. Not gay.

JEN. No, I mean

Do you have a girlfriend or someone you're seeing at the moment?

CHARLIE. Yea. Well not any more. Not since

JEN. And what's her name?

CHARLIE. Does it matter?

JEN. I think so.

CHARLIE. Sadie.

JEN. And what does Sadie do?

CHARLIE. Kids.

> MIKE *snorts*.
>
> No you fucking pervert. I mean she works with kids. In a nursery.
>
> MIKE *raises his hands like 'you said it'*.

JEN. And what does she think about you being here?

CHARLIE. Dunno. Doesn't want to see me no more. Dunno if she knows I'm here.

JEN. And you have a baby on the way?

CHARLIE. Yea.

JEN. And what would you want to tell that baby if you could?

CHARLIE. Not to see me neither.

JEN. And why's that?

> CHARLIE *shrugs*.

CHARLIE. Dunno.

JEN. Yes you do.

CHARLIE. Cos I beat up his mum and she nearly had a miscarriage.

JEN. Okay.

CHARLIE. So it's probably better if I weren't around.

JEN. What if you did things differently? Could your baby see you then?

CHARLIE. He's a he. We're having a boy.

PART TWO, SCENE THREE

JEN. Okay.

CHARLIE. Not okay. All Taylor men are are

,

My grandad beat my nan, my dad beat my mum, I beat Sadie.

JEN. But you're doing something to break that cycle, aren't you?

CHARLIE. Yea, by not being in his life.

JEN. No. By being here. By facing up to what you've done and changing your behaviour, making decisions about your actions going forwards to ensure that you will never

CHARLIE. But how do you know that? How do you know that? How can any of us fucking know that?

JEN. Because you're *here*, because you show up and you talk and

CHARLIE. But I won't always be. This will end and I will be out there and someone at some point will do something to make me furious and that mist will come down and I will hit and kick and stab and so will they, these lot, and so will my son

CHARLIE is on his feet now.

He picks up his plastic chair and throws it on the floor.

It doesn't make the level of noise CHARLIE *was hoping for.*

JEN. Charlie.

He picks it up again and brings it down harder.

A leg snaps off.

CHARLIE. Fuck. Fuck, fuck, fuck, fuck, fuck.

JEN. Charlie!

He continues smashing.

The rest of the group just watch, mesmerised.

CHARLIE. Fuck. Fuck, fuck, fuck, fuck, fuck.

The chair is obliterated.

Scene Four

The men leave.

JEN *sits alone in the circle.*

The wreckage of the chair around her.

FRANK *enters.*

He watches her, unseen, from the back of the room.

Then he walks forwards.

JEN *starts.*

JEN. Frank. Sorry, I didn't

Did you forget something?

FRANK. No, no.

Just wanted a quick word.

JEN. Of course. How can I help?

FRANK. I just wanted to say thank you for everything you've done.

JEN. Oh. That's very, that's nice of you.

FRANK. Yes. It's been an interesting *journey*, and a, a good opportunity for me to reflect on my actions up to this point.

JEN. Well good, I'm glad / you're finding it

FRANK. / But I really don't think I need to stay to finish the programme.

JEN. What? No, you, you need to stay for the full

We've got a whole other module to

FRANK. I came here voluntarily, Jen. My participation in the group isn't mandatory. It's always been the understanding that I can leave these groups whenever I want.

JEN. Well, sort of, but

FRANK. And I think as much as it's been an interesting exercise for me, I'm not convinced it's something I have ever really needed to undertake.

JEN. No, Frank, it really is.

FRANK. Belinda and I have had our ups and downs over the years

JEN. Frank.

FRANK. but no marriage is perfect

JEN. You broke her jaw, three of her fingers and her collarbone. You isolated her from friends, family, work. Locked her in a / cupboard when she

FRANK. / Things I deeply, deeply regret. But after every occasion I have gone through periods of intense reflection and atonement.

JEN. And yet the pattern still continues Frank, which is why you needed to come here.

FRANK. God has been a generous and merciful judge of my past behaviour and it is to Him that I will truly repent.

JEN. And the law? Your faith doesn't give you a free pass to override that.

FRANK. I have been cleared of all misconduct by the appropriate / authorities.

JEN. And what about your wife? What about her?

FRANK. She supports every / decision

JEN. / So that's it, is it? You give up.

FRANK. It's not *giving up*, Jen. I work hard every single day of my life to better myself, to offer myself to the public as a representative of the God which I serve, to care for my flock, my friends, my family.

JEN. And doesn't Belinda deserve your commitment too? Shouldn't she be the person you think of first in this, as the person you've hurt the most?

FRANK. This decision has been made with her and for her. Don't make the mistake of thinking I am here without her support.

JEN. Her *support*. She does whatever you tell her to.

FRANK. I wouldn't underestimate Belinda if I were you.

JEN. Well I obviously underestimated you.

FRANK. Perhaps.

JEN. ,

And there's nothing I can do to change your mind?

FRANK. I'm afraid not. The next session will be my last. I do truly appreciate the work you and the programme have put into our recovery over the past few months

JEN. Hmh.

FRANK. and I wish you, and all of my fellow colleagues, the best in the future. I will explain my decision to them next week. I just wanted to give you the courtesy of telling you first.

JEN. Well that is good of you.

Silence.

FRANK. Perhaps you should give this the same consideration I did. You might just find this isn't for you either.

,

I should go. Belinda's waiting in the car.

,

Goodnight, Jen.

He exits.

The door closes behind him.

There is stillness for a moment.

Then JEN *picks up one of the obliterated chair legs.*

She throws it at the closed door with a cry of rage.

Scene Five

NINA *and* ED*'s house.*

After dinner.

ED. They don't think he knew exactly what it was.

NINA. He's seven, he's not an idiot, Ed.

ED. Well I haven't talked to him about it yet, have you?

NINA. No but

ED. And they haven't had sex education at school yet. Not until Year 6.

NINA. No but they're surrounded by it now, aren't they? It's not like how it was for us. We were so innocent. I had no clue about any of it until I found *The Joy of Sex* on my parents' bookshelf and forced my sister to explain it to me.

ED. Well that's basically the / same

NINA. / Don't you dare. It's nowhere near the same. Watching hardcore pornography is nothing like those seventies drawings of that hairy couple.

ED. It wasn't hardcore

NINA. Ed.

  ED *laughs.*

  Ed! It's not funny.

ED. Sorry, sorry. My parents also had that book. I'd forgotten how hairy they were.

NINA. What do you think, Jen? He'd shown it to this poor little girl in pigtails who was distraught apparently.

JEN. Oh god.

NINA. It did turn out she thought 'that man was murdering that woman'.

ED *stifles a laugh again.*

NINA *whacks him.*

Stop it.

It was quite violent, actually. I'm not surprised.

ED. It wasn't violent. God's sake.

NINA. Well it didn't look very comfortable, that's for sure.

JEN. Where did Oscar get it from?

NINA. Have a guess.

ED. He must have worked out my password.

NINA. For god's sake, Ed.

ED. I didn't realise he even knew where I keep my laptop!

NINA. He plays those little games on it all the time. What were you thinking?

ED. I obviously wasn't. It's not something I would have shown him myself, is it?

NINA. But the worst thing is, they think he was trying to act some of it out on one of the other little girls. The school was really concerned. They used the word *nonconsensual*.

JEN. What?

ED. He didn't know what he was doing.

JEN. Oh my god.

NINA. It obviously wasn't sexual.

JEN. How do you know?

NINA. Because they're not, kids that age aren't aren't

They're too young.

JEN. For god's sake, Nina. You know that's not true.

ED. You're probably right. It's just a bit… *icky* thinking about it.

JEN. Have you talked to him about what happened?

NINA. We've tried but he

He won't talk to *us* about it, so we've

JEN. You can't leave it.

NINA. He won't do it again. We were apoplectic. He knows he's in the dog house.

JEN. But he doesn't know *why*.

ED. Well, I think, I mean he does know

JEN. No. He doesn't. Not really. You have to explain it to him.

ED. All right, Jen. He's not one of your guys. He's a child.

JEN. He is now. But for god's sake, where do you think *my guys* learnt it from?

NINA. Jesus, Jen. You're not seriously saying Oscar's going to turn into a wife beater because of this.

JEN. Why not?

ED. Fucking hell, Jen. You really are getting paranoid.

JEN. Well it doesn't come from nowhere, does it?

He has to understand. It's not his fault. Not yet. But one day he won't be a child any more and what then?

NINA. Jen. You're getting really worked up.

JEN. No I'm not.

ED. You are a bit, mate.

NINA. Sorry, we shouldn't have said anything. We didn't mean to upset you.

JEN. I'm not upset.

She is crying.

I'm just, I'm just, I'm tired and and

NINA. I know.

JEN. You have to talk to him, you have to. You have to explain to him

NINA. All right. Love. All right. We will.

Won't we?

ED. Er, yea.

NINA. We do take this seriously.

JEN. I know, I know I just

NINA. Stay here tonight.

JEN. I can't. I need to

I should go.

NINA. At least let us call you a cab.

JEN. No.

No, I'm fine. I'm just

I need to walk. Clear my head.

She gets up.

Picks up her stuff.

NINA *gets up too.*

NINA (*to* ED). How much have you had to drink? Can you drive her?

ED. Sorry. Definitely too many.

NINA. Me too.

JEN. No, no. I'm fine. Too much wine. Not enough sleep. It's just, it's all been a lot recently.

NINA. Stay here. Please? Just stay. We're worried about you.

JEN. Don't. You don't need to be.

NINA. This job, it just feels

JEN. It's fine. I'm fine.

NINA. After everything that happened with that woman

Jen.

You weren't well. You

She looks at ED.

You still aren't well.

JEN. That has, what happened with Gloria has nothing to do / with this

NINA. / It wasn't your fault. She didn't die because you did / anything wrong

ED. / Nina, don't.

NINA. No, Ed. It's not right. She has to stop, you have to stop blaming yourself for

JEN. I've got to go.

She starts backing out of the room.

NINA. This job won't fix whatever / it is you feel

ED. / Nina.

JEN. / I've got to go

JEN *exits*.

NINA. Jen!   ,

Fuck.

Scene Six

Outside Nina's house.

PETER. Hello.

JEN. Fuck. Peter.

You scared me.

PETER. Sorry.

JEN. What are you

How did you know where I

PETER. I saw you walk past earlier.

JEN. Wait, what?

PETER. I just wanted to, just to see if you wanted to go on another, if you wanted to see each other again.

JEN. We are seeing each other. You're outside my friend's house.

PETER. No I meant, like properly.

JEN. Do you understand how fucking creepy it is that you're here?

PETER. You didn't get back to me. I texted you a few times.

JEN. I've been busy. I thought I'd made it quite clear after last time

PETER. We had sex.

JEN. Yes.

PETER. You don't have sex with people you don't like

JEN. Sometimes you do.

PETER. Let's go somewhere and talk about it. It's freezing.

JEN. No.

PETER. Our local's just round the

JEN. No.

Thank you.

PETER. I deserve an explanation.

JEN. You don't deserve anything.

PETER. You slept with me.

JEN. I know. And then I changed my mind and I told you that.

PETER. But you didn't say why.

JEN. I told you, I'm I'm busy.

PETER. Your friends told you you judge people too quickly. You get scared. Don't give things a chance. Well I think you should give this another chance.

JEN. I'm not scared of this this

　　I don't actually have to explain this to you again. I told you before. I don't see this going any further and I'd like you to respect that.

PETER. But I don't think you know what you want. Not really. Everyone that knows and loves you tells you, why can't you hear it for yourself?

JEN. Because I like being alone. I like being alone more than I like being ambushed outside my friend's door at ten o'clock at night. More than being made to feel guilty or delusional for not feeling the way other people want me to feel.

PETER. Just

　　PETER *takes hold of her arm.*

JEN. Take your hand off me.

PETER. I'm just trying to

JEN. Take your hands off me or I will scream fire.

PETER. You're being ridiculous. Let's just go somewhere and talk about this like / adults

JEN. / FIRE

　　FIRE

　　FIRE

　　FIRE

　　/ FIRE

PETER. / Okay, okay, / okay

JEN. / FIRE

　　FIRE

　　FIRE

FIRE

PETER *exits*.

NINA *enters*.

She sees JEN *and runs to her.*

FIRE

FIRE

FIRE

NINA. Jen. Jen. Jen, it's okay.

It's okay.

NINA *tries to hold her.*

JEN *shakes her off.*

JEN. Can you let me go?

,

Talk to your fucking son.

She exits.

Scene Seven

The group.

MIKE *and* FRANK *bring in chairs and the same circle is formed.*

Two chairs are empty.

MIKE. We'd go six, seven times a year. Not regular. But when we went we knew. We all knew why we were going. It was unspoken but there's a pact. You all know why you're there. The buzz of it, I can't describe it. Knowing, like a secret, what's going to happen. Looking at other people on the train, in your carriage, wondering if they know too.

But you don't do it then.

It's too early.

You need to get a couple of drinks in you first. Oil the engine. Limber up. Safety if nothing else. Your body is more relaxed then. Less likely to get properly hurt if your muscles aren't tense.

And then, I dunno. Something kicks it off. It's not like it's one person, like someone's been nominated to start it. It's more organic than that. You all feel the surge. And maybe, yea, maybe it starts off with one guy punching out another. But that's it. One punch and we're off. We're kicking off. And there's the ones of us that came for it. And then there's the guys that just find themselves in the middle of it and just get stuck in. Caught up in the atmosphere. Barely feeling the fists on you, the kicks.

It's really only the next day it sinks in.

If it's been a particularly bad one.

Coupla mates had a hard time of it.

One

One he

Yea he, well he

Ended up in a wheelchair. Someone stamped on his back. We tried to get him up. But it was a stampede by that point. The police were kettling and this guy, Jase, we couldn't get him up, out of the way.

He's fine now though.

I think.

,

I tried to get it out like that.

But sometimes I got it out at home. And

Yea.

I guess maybe it wasn't very nice to be around.

,

JEN. Thanks Mike.

MIKE. Yea. All right.

JEN. You doing all right?

MIKE. Yea. Definitely.

JEN. Okay. What about, when you were little, what about that?

MIKE. What?

JEN. Did you feel like that then?

MIKE. Guess so.

JEN. And what did you do then?

MIKE. Did the same, I guess.

JEN. Got into fights?

MIKE. Yea.

JEN. Where?

MIKE. Where?

JEN. Where.

MIKE. Playground. Playing fields after school. Sport. I dunno.

JEN. Okay.

MIKE. Clubs when I got older. The guys in there. One guy at work I used to, out the back. Sometimes my sister when we were younger. Sometimes when we got older too.

JEN. When?

MIKE. Um. When our parents had gone out.

JEN. Just then?

MIKE. Sometimes at night. When they were asleep.

JEN. Do you think they knew?

   MIKE *shakes his head*.

MIKE. No.

,

Sometimes

,

Sometimes I hoped they would find out cos then maybe they'd

,

But they never did so

,

,

One of his lot knew.

He points at FRANK.

They knew. She used to be in the choir and she told one of them. And when I was sixteen and she was fourteen she put scissors in her wrists and got in the bath. And after, this guy, one of his lot, just said 'Sorry for your loss'. And gave me this knowing look. But he didn't say anything. Didn't say anything before and didn't say anything after.

,

,

Where's Charlie?

JEN. I don't know. So how do you feel about

MIKE. He doesn't miss these. He's not like that.

FRANK. Maybe he's ill.

MIKE. He'd've fucking called if he was ill, Frank.

JEN. Back on track.

FRANK. Maybe, yes.

MIKE. What?

FRANK. I was agreeing with you.

MIKE. Too right.

JEN. Come on, let's not worry about Charlie. I'm sure there's a good explanation. We're not done with

MIKE. I mean this is ridiculous. Dropping like flies round here. Just you and me now, Frank. That's a fucking joke.

FRANK. Well actually

JEN. Not now, Frank.

MIKE. Eh?

FRANK. Have you heard anything about Brian's case?

JEN. No.

MIKE. Just trying to see those kids.

JEN. Yes, well

MIKE. Yes well nothing. Might not be his kids by blood, but he raised them like his own. Isn't right to take them away.

JEN. Well, we don't know all of the facts, do we?

MIKE. Your kids still see you, Frank?

FRANK. None of your business.

MIKE. That's a no then.

JEN. Watch it, Mike.

MIKE. Just saying.

FRANK. Well don't.

MIKE. Funny you still wear that that

He motions FRANK*'s dog collar.*

Can't surely still be a man of the cloth after

JEN. Mike.

MIKE. Bit fucking tragic you still put it on each day. When I know for a fact you got struck off / years ago.

FRANK. / You're a nasty piece of work, Mike. You know that?

MIKE. It has been said.

What is it with you, Frank? What's your excuse? I still can't work it out. Charlie's here because of his dad, Brian's a virgin. Was a virgin. I've got 'anger issues' apparently. What are you?

JEN. I'm going to ask you to leave now, Mike.

MIKE. You got all that suppressed rage in you, haven't you? Where's that come from? You get fiddled at Bible camp did you?

JEN. That's it. Mike, get out!

FRANK *launches himself at* MIKE.

MIKE, *laughing, side steps him and* FRANK *falls to the floor.*

Out!

Frank.

JEN *goes to* FRANK.

Helps him up.

Are you okay?

(*To* MIKE.) Out, now!

But MIKE *is looking towards the door.*

CHARLIE *enters.*

There is blood down his front.

He walks in slowly.

The commotion of before dies out as they turn and see him enter.

CHARLIE. I

I

MIKE. Charlie.

CHARLIE. I just went to see if he was okay. I brought him some of the banana bread I made.

MIKE. What happened?

CHARLIE. He's dead. Brian. He's

She wasn't going to let him see the little ones and

He was going to prison for

Because of the restraining order.

He broke the restraining order.

FRANK. So he killed himself?

CHARLIE. Them first.

He killed them all first.

,

I just went round to give him some banana bread.

Scene Eight

JEN *sits in the circle of chairs alone.*

A cake tin on her lap.

She reaches inside and pulls out some millionaire shortbread.

Bites into it.

Chews.

NINA *appears at the open door behind her.*

She watches JEN *for a moment.*

She knocks.

JEN *looks around.*

NINA. Only me.

JEN. Hi.

NINA. I was just

I was passing.

JEN. No you weren't.

NINA. No I wasn't.

,

Can I

She motions to one of the empty chairs.

JEN *nods.*

NINA *sits.*

What you got there?

JEN. Millionaire shortbread.

NINA. Oh go on.

JEN *offers her the tin.*

NINA *takes out a shortbread and eats.*

Christ alive that's good.

JEN. I know. One of the wives makes it.

NINA. Perks of the job, eh?

JEN. Too many to count.

They sit, eating in silence for a moment.

NINA. I don't know why, I thought it would be a bit more... *jail*-like.

They buzzed me right in.

JEN. That's probably concerning.

NINA. It's actually quite nice here.

Considering.

JEN. Hmh.

NINA. Aren't there usually more people though?

JEN. Ha ha.

No. No one's turned up.

She looks at her watch.

Unsurprisingly.

NINA. Good job I popped by then. I was just going to leave you this

She takes an envelope out of her pocket.

but then they said at reception you were in here all Billy No Mates so

JEN. What is it?

NINA. Oh no, you can't read it now.

JEN *tries to grab the envelope.*

NINA *snatches it away.*

JEN. Gimme.

NINA. No!

JEN. Gimme!

JEN *grabs it.*

Opens the envelope.

NINA *looks embarrassed.*

NINA. I've been meaning to

You were right. About Oscar.

JEN. You wrote me a letter?

NINA. I wasn't sure if

I didn't know if you wanted to see me.

JEN. A handwritten letter?

NINA. It's stupid, I

JEN. Like when we were ten and you decapitated my Beanie Baby and your mum made you write me a note to apologise?

NINA. Well it worked, didn't it?

JEN smiles.

Starts to read.

We spoke to him. Properly this time. Spoke to his teacher too. She gave us a pamphlet.

JEN. Christ.

NINA. *What to do when your son's becoming a sex pest.*

JEN. Catchy.

NINA. Ed's going on a course.

JEN. What?

NINA. Yea. A parenting course. You scared the shit out of him.

JEN. No I didn't.

NINA. Yea. He said it's time he 'learnt to communicate better with the kids'.

JEN. Bloody hell.

NINA. I know.

,

He's been teaching me about feminism too which is great.

JEN laughs.

JEN. Good old Ed.

Tears roll suddenly down JEN's face.

NINA squeezes her hand.

NINA. I'm sorry about what I said too. About the job.

JEN. No, you were right. I can't do this. Another woman dead and it's my fault again, it's my

NINA. Wh–

JEN. I kicked him off. I sent him back out into the world when he was completely

NINA. Hey now. Whatever it

Whatever's happened. It's not your

You were just doing your job.

JEN. I did the same to Gloria. The woman I

I pushed them both away.

It's my fault

NINA. Of course it's / not

JEN. / I told her, I told her, I told her she was fucking spineless. That I couldn't help her unless she helped herself. That I was sick of coming round and hearing her excuses for him. And then I left and he killed her.

NINA. Oh, Jen.

JEN. He killed her and I will never, ever forgive myself for that.

NINA holds her tightly.

NINA. You don't

Don't really think that it's your

,

Do you?

The women break apart.

JEN *looks at her, unsure.*

MIKE *appears in the doorway.*

MIKE. Um

They look around.

JEN *composes herself quickly.*

JEN. Mike.

MIKE. All right?

JEN. Sorry, this is

This is Nina.

Nina, this is

,

MIKE. Mike?

JEN. Yea, sorry I didn't

Confidentiality.

MIKE. You already said my name.

NINA. Nice to meet you, Mike.

MIKE. Likewise.

,

Sorry are we not

Tonight. Is there no

JEN. Oh no, there

Yea, no there is. I just wasn't sure anyone was coming.

MIKE. Yea, sorry, I couldn't

My lift didn't show so I had to

On the bus, you know.

JEN. Yea. Yea, no it's fine.

Pause.

NINA *looks uncomfortable.*

NINA. Well I'm just

I was about to leave. Just came for the shortbread so

She gets up.

Squeezes JEN*'s shoulder as she walks past.*

I'll come and pick you up. Later.

JEN *nods*.

NINA *and* MIKE *pass each other.*

They share a momentary look.

A second where MIKE *is* ED *and* ED *is* MIKE.

Then it's over.

Cheers then.

She exits.

MIKE *approaches.*

He sits down.

MIKE. That from Belinda?

JEN. Yea. Want some?

MIKE. Are you kidding? I'm fucking gluten intolerant, Jen.

JEN. Sorry.

They laugh.

MIKE. Anyway. Trying to avoid sugar. Charlie keeps bringing me round gluten-free banana bread he's made. It's fucking crack that stuff. I'm having to wean myself off.

JEN. Wow.

MIKE. I know. You'd think he'd be over making it after

,

Think he's just making sure none of the rest of us have

You know.

JEN. Poor Charlie.

MIKE. He'll be all right.

,

You all right?

PART TWO, SCENE EIGHT

JEN. Yea.

You?

MIKE. Yea.

,

Look I know it's not much of a group if it's just me and I thought maybe I wouldn't come back but I was at home and and

Cos I like the noise. My place is

Too quiet. I need the... bullshit. Hubbub.

Charlie's stupid fucking comments.

Frank's twattery.

Brian's

,

So, you know, if there's

JEN. Yea.

Yea, I mean of course. There's actually a new group starting later tonight. We got an extension on the funding to run another one. Found out just before

,

So if you wanted to stay for that? Then next week maybe you and Charlie could

MIKE. Charlie won't come.

JEN. No. Maybe not.

MIKE. He's doing all right though.

JEN. Yea?

MIKE. Trying out being a dad on me I reckon.

JEN. That's nice.

MIKE. It's unbearable.

He laughs.

I think he just needs to do it now. You know. All this stuff. Out there.

Put it into practice.

JEN. Right. Well

Good for him.

,

And you?

MIKE. Ah, you know me. I'm a group kinda guy. I thrive in these sorts of things.

JEN. Right.

She laughs.

MIKE. I'm not ready to leave yet.

JEN. That's okay. That's good.

I wouldn't have signed you off anyway.

MIKE. Ha, well there you go.

Silence.

JEN. I don't know if I'll stay though. Just so you know. I think maybe I

Maybe it's time I moved on.

MIKE. Huh.

JEN. You know, because there's

So much of the world I haven't

So much of the UK even.

MIKE. Sure yea.

JEN. And I'm

Never been sure what I want to do. Not too late to retrain. Try something totally different.

I'm still relatively young and

MIKE. You're not that young, Jen.

JEN. Huh.

,

,

I just don't think I'll ever get over this.

MIKE. ,

Good.

It's fucking awful.

It's the worst possible thing.

,

Look, I know you think you've fucked up somehow. And maybe you did. But with the best will in the world, Jen it's actually not about you.

It's not about you at all.

It's about us. *Learning, changing, doing the work.* And you can help us with that but you can't take

JEN. responsibility for it.

Silence.

JEN *and* MIKE *look out.*

They can't look at each other.

MIKE. Besides, the fuck else are you gonna do? Become a yoga teacher?

She laughs.

He takes her hand.

A moment of connection that she allows to happen.

Then it's broken.

She stands up and shakes herself off. Professional again.

JEN. I'd be a terrible yoga teacher. Zero flexibility.

MIKE. I started yoga actually.

JEN. Did you?

MIKE. Well. Put on a video with that bendy YouTube Texan and lasted five minutes. Can't stand Americans.

JEN. Well that's

Fair enough.

,

Thank you.

MIKE. Yea.

A comfortable silence.

JEN. Want to give me a hand putting more chairs out? Quite a big group starting tonight.

They actually upped our funding this time.

MIKE. Yea?

,

All right then.

In silence they put out more white chairs. The circle is expanded.

SIOBHAN *enters and stands to one side watching them work.*

Time passes.

The other actors enter the space as new participants.

The sound of male voices chatting gets louder and louder.

JEN *stands before them.*

JEN. Okay then.

The voices quieten.

Let's get started.

Blackout.

A Nick Hern Book

Bindweed first published in Great Britain as a paperback original in 2024 by Nick Hern Books Limited, The Glasshouse, 49a Goldhawk Road, London W12 8QP, in association with the Mercury Theatre, Colchester co-produced by HighTide and the New Wolsey, in association with the Royal Exchange Theatre

Bindweed copyright © 2024 Martha Loader

Martha Loader has asserted her right to be identified as the author of this work

Cover artwork by Matthew Smith at Desk Tidy Design

Designed and typeset by Nick Hern Books, London
Printed in Great Britain by Mimeo Ltd, Huntingdon, Cambridgeshire PE29 6XX

A CIP catalogue record for this book is available from the British Library

ISBN 978 1 83904 366 6

CAUTION All rights whatsoever in this play are strictly reserved. Requests to reproduce the text in whole or in part should be addressed to the publisher.

Amateur Performing Rights Applications for performance, including readings and excerpts, by amateurs in the English language should be addressed to the Performing Rights Manager, Nick Hern Books, The Glasshouse, 49a Goldhawk Road, London W12 8QP, *tel* +44 (0)20 8749 4953, *email* rights@nickhernbooks.co.uk, except as follows:

Australia: ORiGiN Theatrical, *tel* +61 (2) 8514 5201,
email enquiries@originmusic.com.au, *web* www.origintheatrical.com.au

New Zealand: Play Bureau, 20 Rua Street, Mangapapa, Gisborne 4010,
tel +64 21 258 3998, *email* info@playbureau.com

United States of America and Canada: Creative Artists Agency, see details below

Professional Performing Rights Rights Applications for performance by professionals in any medium and in any language throughout the world should be addressed in the first instance to Creative Artists Agency, 12 Hammersmith Grove, Hammersmith, London W6 7AP, *tel* +44 (0)20 8846 3000, *fax* +1 212 277 9099, *email* rhiannon.williams@caa.com

No performance of any kind may be given unless a licence has been obtained. Applications should be made before rehearsals begin. Publication of this play does not necessarily indicate its availability for amateur performance.

www.nickhernbooks.co.uk/environmental-policy